HM
206
C35

Carey, George Warren, 1927-
    Teaching population geography; an inter-
disciplinary ecological approach [by]
George W. Carey [and] Julie Schwartzberg.
New York, Teachers College Press [1969]
    134 p. maps. (Social studies sources)
    "An annotated bibliography": p. 37-102.
    Includes bibliographical references.
    1. Human ecology - Study and teaching.
2. Demography - Study and teaching.
3. Human ecology - Bibl. 4. Demography -
Bibl.   I. Schwartzberg,
Julie, joint   author. II. Title.

SOCIAL
STUDIES
SOURCES

Erling M. Hunt, Series Editor

Congress and the President:
Readings in Executive-Legislative Relations
by Walter Earl Travis

A Bibliography for Teachers of Social Studies
by Raymond A. Ducharme, Jr., Joseph Katz, and
Arthur D. Sheekey

Honors Teaching in American History
by Lawrence A. Fink

American History Through Conflicting Interpretations
by David F. Kellum

Charles A. Beard and the Social Studies: A Book of Readings
by Raymond A. Ducharme, Jr.

Teaching Population Geography
by George W. Carey and Julie Schwartzberg

TEACHING POPULATION GEOGRAPHY

An Interdisciplinary Ecological Approach

GEORGE W. CAREY

JULIE SCHWARTZBERG

Social Studies Sources
Erling M. Hunt, Series Editor

TEACHERS COLLEGE PRESS

Teachers College, Columbia University
New York, New York

Sources of Illustrations, Chapter IV.

Figure 1. From Glenn T. Trewartha, "New Population Maps of Uganda, Kenya, Nyasaland, and Gold Coast," *Annals of the Association of American Geographers,* 47 (1957), Fig. 5. Map by Gene E. Musolf. Reproduced by courtesy of the *Annals of the Association of American Geographers.*

Figure 2. From George F. Jenks, "Generalization in Statistical Mapping," *Annals of the Association of American Geographers,* 53 (1963), 18, Fig. 5. Reproduced by courtesy of the *Annals of the Association of American Geographers.*

Figure 3. The authors.

Figure 4. From R. K. Udo, "Disintegration of Nucleated Settlement in Eastern Nigeria, *Geographical Review,* 55 (1965), 55, Fig. 2. Reproduced by courtesy of the *Geographical Review.*

Figure 5. From Arthur H. Robinson, "Mapping the Correspondence of Isarithmic Maps," *Annals of the Association of American Geographers,* 52 (1962), 418, Fig. 3A. Reproduced by courtesy of the *Annals of the Association of American Geographers.*

Figure 6. The authors.

Figure 7. From Prodyumna P. Karan, "Changes in Indian Industrial Location," *Annals of the Association of American Geographers,* 54 (1964), 344, Fig. 5. Reproduced by courtesy of the *Annals of the Association of American Geographers.*

Figure 8. From Roy Chung, *Space-Time Diffusion of the Transition Model: Twentieth Century Patterns.* Unpublished paper, presented at the Annual Meetings of the Population Association of America, New York, 1966. Used with the author's permission.

Figures 9–12. The authors.

Cover design by Gaspar Vilato

Manufactured in the United States of America

Authors' Introduction

The questions of "overpopulation" and "underpopulation" are grave concerns of modern society. In the popular press and the information media, the term "population explosion" has gained great currency, as has the specter of a Malthusian destiny for the world.

This work is intended to provide the thoughtful teacher with some suggestions and some techniques for introducing population study to the student in terms of concrete case studies which explore the relationship between population and the carrying capacity of an environment in terms less cataclysmic than those of Malthusian determinism. For there are instances, in human societies and animal societies as well, where a functional equilibrium has been established through means other than the classical starvation and predation cycles. This is not to say that mankind need not concern itself with demographic planning. Rather we suggest that there exist a number of useful points of intervention in human ecology where equilibrating pressures may be applied—in other words, there are a diversity of weapons in the armory of population control ranging from technical control devices to more subtle social constraints.

The manuscript was written under the sponsorship of The Population Council, with the financial support of the Population Instructional Materials Project, and the authors thank Dr. Sloan R. Wayland, the project director, for his guidance and counsel. Another vote of thanks goes to the American Geographical Society, and its courtesy in making its unparalleled regional research library and map collection available to our use. Finally we would like to express our appreciation to Carolyn Rhodes, Maria Morales, and Juanita Armelin for their help in preparing the manuscript.

G. W. C.
J. S.

Contents

TEACHING POPULATION GEOGRAPHY

I. Demography, Human Ecology, and Geography

Geography as a school subject is taught widely all over the world. In the main, it is presented to students under either a regional or a topical plan of organization, or some combination of the two. The topical approach customarily systematizes world spatial patterns of phenomena significant to man under categories such as *climate, terrain, drainage, political spheres of influence, economic spheres of influence, population, urbanization,* or the like. The regional approach, on the other hand, divides up the earth's surface into a number of entities called *regions* and *subregions,* and for each one of these, inquires in depth as to how the various topical dimensions of the region are present, spatially differentiated and interrelated. Most geographers would probably agree that whether one considers oneself a regional or topical specialist is largely a matter of emphasis. The topical climatologist, for example, finds it useful to define world climate regions in pursuing his end of understanding climate, while the regional specialist interested in Africa, for example, often finds it useful to subdivide that continent by climate regions in order to pursue his end of understanding the complexity of man-land relationships that pertain to his region of interest.

Geography has long since outgrown environmental determinism. No longer can it be accepted, any more than other crude forms of Social Darwinism can in any other of the social sciences. Owing to the work of such geographers as Brunhes, Vidal de la Blache, and Demangeon, for example, we are aware that man shapes his environment as much as he is shaped by it. Indeed, in the contemporary world, where urban environments especially can be called more man-made than natural, environmental determinism becomes particularly difficult for the urban geographer to accept.

HUMAN GEOGRAPHY AND DEMOGRAPHY

While geography is so often concerned with the man-environment relationship, demography has a somewhat narrower outlook. It is con-

1

cerned with the dynamics of population change, and with other phenomena as they bear upon population change. By "the dynamics of population change," we refer to vital statistics, such as birth and death rates, their analysis, and trends in these variables, as well as the changing age and sex structure of the population, and patterns and trends in migration. The work of the demographer in the "narrow" sense is largely concerned with these aspects of population study, and in order to project changes for planning purposes, he is often concerned with evolving sophisticated and specialized statistical techniques in order to make his projections of increasingly greater reliability. A demographer who takes the "wide" view of his field is concerned not only with population dynamics *per se,* but also with how the organization of society itself in its setting often alters these apparently purely biological phenomena of birth and death. Among the earliest scholars to call attention to the relationships between population dynamics and society was Maurice Halbwachs, who brings forward convincing arguments showing that sex composition, population distribution, birth and death rates, and the overall rise or decline of populations along with their age compositions are all related to social factors, and are partly to be observed in peculiarities of geographical distribution.

We must recognize that both the equilibrium among these [population age] groups and their succession—i.e., the movement by which one generation succeeds another—result from the organization of society, rather than exclusively or even primarily from biological forces and laws.[1]

Insofar as the study of the organization of society must include the environment, the discipline of demography in the wide sense is greatly interested in the work of the geographer, though it must also be recognized that there is at least one fundamental difference in outlook as well —the geographer, interested in the man-environment relationship as it varies over the surface of the earth, feels free to concentrate his attention on dimensions of the natural environment (physical geography) or even upon man-made landscapes rather than on purely human distributions, while the demographer has his attention always focused upon population as the object of his study.

It is thus improper to suggest that demography could replace geography in the school curriculum, yet insofar as human geography concentrates upon the "man" term of the man-environment relationship, it is of great potential value to the geography teacher and can provide a valuable addition to the resources of the teacher in the classroom. Population dynamics, or demography in the "narrow" sense, can usefully be inserted into the topical structure of geography in the same manner as climatology and economic geography, while demography in the wider sense may be used to enrich depth studies of world regions. Since material for the teacher oriented towards population dynamics already exists,[2] this work will concern itself primarily with the study of population in the wider sense—as it is related to its total environment—social as well as physical.

THE PERSPECTIVE OF HUMAN ECOLOGY

The field of human ecology, as it has developed in the twentieth century, essentially owes its existence to the fact that each of the separate social science disciplines offers only a limited although intense and specialized view of human society and culture. The fuller model of any community must take into account the findings of the sociologist, the anthropologist, the political scientist, the demographer, the geographer, the historian, and the economist, along with those of scholars in all the other related social and behavioral science disciplines. Human ecology therefore focuses upon the social community as the object of study rather than upon any single academic discipline, recognizing that the interplay between men and their environment is modified by the outlook, organization, and technical attainments that they possess. It is beyond the scope of this work to detail the development of human ecology, but the reader is referred to the voluminous literature on the subject.[3]

One helpful synthesis of the various threads of interpretation within human ecology is provided by Gist and Fava.[4] A human society consists of a population residing in an environment. The manner in which the population lives is exclusively related neither to the sheer number of people, nor to their population dynamics, nor to the range of choices of potential resources present in the environment. It is related also to the technology possessed by the society, the manner in which the society is organized, and the way in which the society perceives its environment. All of these factors—population, environment, technology, organization, and social psychology—in balance describe the relationship between the human community and its environment.

Consider the coking coal fields underlying the Appalachian Plateau of Pennsylvania in the United States, for instance.[5] It is all too easy to assert that steelmaking activities were bound to locate there, owing to the presence in the environment of an essential resource. During the period of time when American Indian cultures were dominant in that region, the technology of the Indian society did not include steelmaking in its repertoire, nor was the society organized around a politico-

3

economic system conducive to the rapid elaboration of metallurgical technology. Furthermore, although seams of coal were readily visible to their eyes, the Indian perception of the environment—their world view, as it were—consigned coal to the category of undifferentiated rock.

This is not to say, necessarily, that the Indians of western Pennsylvania were of a lower order of culture than the residents of modern Pittsburgh. They possessed techniques and skills related to survival in the aboriginal woodlands and the perception of innumerable useful forest "resources" that the modern Pennsylvanian has lost. Furthermore, although modern Pittsburgh abounds with goods, services, transportation and communications facilities, and a socio-political structure which the Indian would be at a loss to fathom, to a certain extent the reverse is also true. Certainly the processes by which modern Pittsburgh has grown have altered the environment far more than the Indian did. Yet this alteration includes, to an alarming extent, a systematic poisoning of the natural surroundings by pollutants.

These dimensions, or poles of reference, relevant to the study of human communities—population, organization, technology, environment, and world view (or social psychology)—are usually inextricably interrelated. Let there be a change in any one, and, as gears turn other gears, the whole system will change and adjust. A new population migrating into an area (the ecologist sometimes says *invading* the area) may very well bring with it an outlook, organization, and technology of its own which will completely change the community.

A handful of Spaniards under Cortes and his followers had such an impact upon the Valley of Central Mexico.[6] The organization of society was changed: the Spanish hegemony replaced the Aztec, and the Catholic religion was propagated. Spanish family institutions became the norm for the ruling class. A cash and commercial economy based upon metallurgy and commercial agriculture replaced the Indian barter economy. The technology of metallurgy, in turn, made further conquest easier, and the innovation of the printing press facilitated the process of culture change, fostering the spread of the Spanish language as a vehicle for culture. The world view of the people changed, in turn, as Mexico City became a commercial pivot for trade between the far East and Spain. Yet the incoming population of Spaniards was changed as much as it effected change.

Mexican Catholicism absorbed much from the rites and rituals of the Aztecs. Gradually the organization of Mexican society drifted far away from that of Spain sufficiently to create a sense of Mexican solidarity and identity, in the context of which the Spaniard was regarded as a foreigner. The selective migration of Spaniards to the New World, being

4

male, led inevitably to a considerable amount of intermarriage and concubinage. The children born of such unions had neither the Spanish nor the Indian outlook, but a fusion of the two with perhaps even more influence from the mother than from the father.

In the context of this all-too-sketchy discussion, the geographer is particularly interested in the adjustments of the *environment* to the change initiated by the Spanish invasion, while the demographer is interested in the *population* changes within the Mexican valley.

During the Aztec period a condition of equilibrium—or balance of population with resources—seems to have prevailed in the Valley. The Aztecs lived on a series of islands in the midst of a lake (Lake Texcoco) and along the shore. Many of the islands were artificial, constructed of mud and wicker rafts floated into position, sunk and built up above water level. These islands were used to raise agricultural produce. Since the lake was saline, fresh water was brought along an earthwork causeway from Chapultepec to the main islands, on which the Aztec city of Tenochtitlán was located. The population lived in communities of extended families and commuted to their island farming activities by boat. Human wastes from the city and villages, instead of being permitted to pollute the lake, were collected, sun-dried, purified, and used as fertilizer.

Since this regime was a relatively healthy one, one may wonder at the fact that the population remained in equilibrium instead of expanding in a Malthusian fashion to bring ultimate imbalance and disaster. A partial explanation for this phenomenon is afforded by the fact that, politically, the Aztecs were organized into a theocratic state, and many of the religious observances demanded human sacrifice. Thus it was a regular religious institutional observance among Aztec cities to engage in internicine war for the purpose of gaining captives to sacrifice. This reduced the young male population considerably, since heroic achievements in these wars were the vehicle to improved social rank and status, and many young men died or were captured and sacrificed in the efforts to excel. Many youths died before procreating—the right to bear arms was proferred at sixteen years of age, but the right to marry was withheld until twenty. Although on certain occasions children and young women were sacrificed, young men were the principal victims. On one occasion in 1498, no fewer than twenty thousand victims were given up to the gods. In addition to controlling population numbers, these activities produced a gross surplus of females in the population. Under the circumstances, polygyny was practiced. These periodic decimations, along with occasional disasters such as the crop failures from 1451 to 1456, served, however grisly the mechanism may appear, to keep the population at equilibrium. It must be borne in mind, nonetheless, that

5

from the world view of the participants in the sacrifice cult, they were engaged in a holy and ennobling work, and those sacrificed were guaranteed immortality.

With the Spanish occupation of the valley, these practices were ended in the name of humanity. The results might well have been predicted: the Aztec population "exploded" in the post-conquest years, and the level of living among the Indians diminished to bare subsistence. While the Spanish classes had a world-wide environment to draw upon for support through trade and commerce, the unchecked Indian population had to subsist upon the fast-exhausted agricultural resources of the Valley of Mexico.

Inevitably, to the interest of the geographer, the environment changed too. The Spanish, intent on changing Aztec Tenochtitlán to Hispanic Mexico City, razed the older city and began the process of filling in Lake Texcoco. The Spanish "perception" of a great city was a settlement with broad plazas upon which the church confronted public buildings, connected by wide avenues. In order to lay out a city of the size and scale demanded by the functions of the capital of New Spain, the salt lake had to be filled in. So it was that fresh water was brought into the city via underground conduit. In Tenochtitlán, wastes had been returned to the soil by way of reclamation as fertilizer; in Mexico City they were disposed of in latrines or in the street, poisoning the soil. As the Spanish buildings began to sink on the filled-in and unstable lake bottom, they ruptured the aging fresh water conduits, and contaminants from the poisoned soil seeped in, laying the preconditions for the spread of urban pestilence. Modern Mexico City is still beset with water supply problems arising from the days of the Viceroyalty of New Spain.

This brief example shows us the population and the environment of the Valley of Mexico under two contrasting conditions of equilibrium. In the first case religious and social controls maintained the population at equilibrium through apparently inhumane human sacrifice and ritual war at a relatively ample subsistence level. In the second case, under a different technology, organization, and world view, the rural population rose to the Malthusian limit of local productivity and reached equilibrium through the environmental mechanisms of starvation and infant death, while the urban population was controlled by pestilence.

AN ECOLOGICAL MODEL

In every society we may consider the following model to apply. Each vertex of the pentagon shown below represents one of the ecological dimensions, while the lines connecting the vertices mean that a change in any one elicits changes in all. The arrows labelled *inputs* and *outputs* show that the typical human ecological system is not a closed system. Population enters it and leaves it bringing or removing skills, needs, or demands. Economically, religiously, and politically, influences enter and leave the system as policies promulgated in political or religious capitals or in economic centers affect the community. Likewise, commercial, religious, and political institutions within the ecological community make their decisions felt elsewhere. In the same ways, through books, radio, or the press, new outlooks developed in one community enter others, altering their world-view. In the sphere of the environment, air, water, and sunlight must enter, and wastes must be disposed of. It is crucial that wastes be not disposed of in such a way as to poison the air or water entering other communities.

Human Ecological System

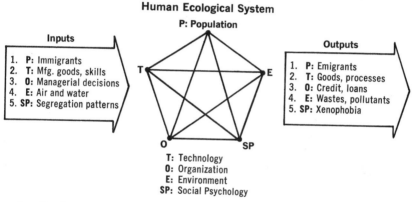

P: Population

Inputs

1. **P:** Immigrants
2. **T:** Mfg. goods, skills
3. **O:** Managerial decisions
4. **E:** Air and water
5. **SP:** Segregation patterns

Outputs

1. **P:** Emigrants
2. **T:** Goods, processes
3. **O:** Credit, loans
4. **E:** Wastes, pollutants
5. **SP:** Xenophobia

T: Technology
O: Organization
E: Environment
SP: Social Psychology

As all of these inputs enter and outputs leave the human ecological system, if the net effect is to maintain a constant population at about the same level of life, it may be said that the system is in a kind of dynamic equilibrium or balance called a steady-state. The ways in which the inputs are processed, distributed, and consumed and in which the outputs are dispatched are intimately related to the layout of the community and clearly reflected in the human geography of the region—the kind and arrangement of transportation arteries, houses, commercial buildings, public utility facilities, and institutions for public information and amusement. The demographer is concerned about whether the population is in equilibrium or in disequilibrium, and whether a satisfactory equilibrium may be achieved through benign technological and social organizational controls, involving a modified social psychological outlook rather than Malthusian controls of famine and pestilence. The human geographer's interest frequently coincides with the demographer's.

We shall present, in Chapter Two, subcategories of the five ecological dimensions, with suggestions as to how they may be used for instruction and analysis, and then three case studies showing the relationships of population equilibrium and disequilibrium to these dimensions. Chapter Three will consist of an annotated bibliography of useful material on our theme in English, and Chapter Four will discuss audio-visual aids as they may be used in the classroom to implement the study of demographic-geographic systems.

NOTES

[1] Maurice Halbwachs, *Population and Society* (published originally in Paris, 1938, tr. Otis Dudley Duncan and Harold W. Pfantz). Glencoe, Illinois: Free Press, 1960, p. 131.

[2] Hazel W. Hertzberg, *Teaching Population Dynamics: An Instructional Unit for Secondary School Students.* New York: Population Instructional Materials Project, International Studies Program, Teachers College, Columbia University, 1965.

[3] Particularly useful are the following: Amos Hawley, *Human Ecology* (New York: Ronald Press, 1950); Otis D. Duncan, "Human Ecology and Population Studies," *in* Philip M. Hauser and Otis D. Duncan (eds.), *The Study of Population* (Chicago: University of Chicago Press, 1959); George A. Theodorson, *Studies in Human Ecology* (New York: Harper and Row, 1961); and James A. Quinn, *Human Ecology* (Englewood Cliffs, N. J.: Prentice-Hall, 1950). Leo F. Schnore, in Chapter 1 of *The Urban Scene* (New York: Free Press, 1965), gives a particularly cogent and valuable analysis of the status of human ecology in the sociological tradition. See also Harlan H. Barrows, "Geography as Human Ecology," *Annals, Association of American Geographers,* 13:1–13, March 1923.

[4] Noel P. Gist and Sylvia Fleis Fava, *Urban Society.* New York: Thomas Y. Crowell Company, 1964, pp. 95–117.

[5] The authors are indebted to Prof. H. Phillip Bacon of the Geography Department, University of Washington, for interesting them in this example and, as well, in the case study of the M'zab that follows in Chapter 2.

[6] Much of the factual material in the case description of the Valley of Central Mexico is drawn from George C. Vaillant, *The Aztecs of Mexico* (New York: Doubleday, Doran and Company, 1941). It is reorganized and reinterpreted in the context of human ecology.

II. Three Case Studies

The M'zab, the Irish Famine, and Morrisville, Pennsylvania

The three cases which we shall briefly consider in this chapter comprise, in turn, a case of demographic equilibrium in a comparatively isolated community; a case of demographic disequilibrium and population decline by "death control"; and a case of demographic changes attending urbanization. Before the cases are treated, it will be necessary to set forth a more detailed framework within which the population changes can be explored.

THE FRAME OF REFERENCE

Since population makeup and population change are related to technology, organization, social psychology, and environment, as we established in Chapter One, before describing an exemplary case it is often helpful to organize the pertinent data with respect to those dimensions.

Population

Much information about specific regions and communities may be collected from sources discussed in the bibliography, Chapter Three. Among the significant and frequently sought data on populations are the following:

1. Size.
2. Sex makeup.
3. Age makeup.
4. Vital statistics: birth rates, death rates, rates of increase or decrease, migration data.
5. Makeup according to various cultural categories: family, marriage and divorce, educational level, ethnic origin, employment, and so forth.
6. Trends with time in all the above.
7. Reliability of the data, usually related to methods and frequency of census-taking and data collection.

Since Hertzberg[1] covers much of this ground from an educational viewpoint, we do not treat this area *in extenso* here.

9

Environment

The geographer traditionally is well equipped to analyze regional environments in terms of the resources they offer, if the modern dynamic concept of resource[2] is always intended. In the older view, a region might be likened to a cabinet with a fixed, limited, and absolute inventory of contents which, if utilized, can never be replaced. The more dynamic view recognizes that a non-resource in one period may become a resource in the next. Given the invention of a commercial process for refining aluminum, bauxite—a previously useless clay—becomes an important resource. Deposits of "rock" become deposits of "ore." And as synthetics come into use, it is conceivable that the position of even wood and metal in the resource realm may change.

Some resources are renewable and some non-renewable, yet under economic and demographic pressures, advances in methods of reclamation and recycling may convert more resources into the renewable category. Suppose a population is confronted with a vast, sparsely occupied continent, as happened to the people of the United States in the early nineteenth century. In their social psychology, abundant land may come to be regarded as inexhaustible and hence may be drained of its productive power as the farmer feels free to abandon it and move on to virgin territory. Land is thus regarded as an inexhaustible, non-renewable resource. Once the population is confronted by a land shortage and overall soil depletion problems, its perception of the use of the soil may change, inducing policy changes in society directed to the renewal and regeneration of ravaged farmland—in some cases, perhaps, too late. This suggests that "natural resources" in the environment of a society are not independent, absolute quantities but are themselves related to the other main variables of population, technology, organization, and social psychology.

In compiling data on the environment of a society, it is often useful to categorize it under systematic headings such as the ones below:

(1) Climate: temperature, pressure, humidity, precipitation, wind and storm, and climatic accident information.

(2) Land forms, including the relative arrangement of land in various classes of slope, relief, and altitude: classes of shoreline, drainage basins, and so forth.

(3) Soils: zonal, intrazonal, and azonal types and occurrences.

(4) Biotic resources: plants and animals for food and other use and their natural enemies.

(5) Mineral resources: water, fuel minerals, fissionable materials, other minerals (both metallic and non-metallic).

(6) Location: the relationship of the region of study with contiguous regions that provide inputs or receive outputs.

Technology

The technology practiced in a region has a direct bearing on the carrying capacity of that region—that is, on the population that can be supported at a socially acceptable level of subsistence. Clearly, an agricultural region exploited carefully under an optimum regime of soil and water conservation, with the scientific farming of the crops best calculated to be productive, supports more people comfortably than a region rudely used for subsistence farming. Indeed, much of the population supported under the careful regime may be free to work away from the farm at urban jobs providing other necessary goods and services. It will be noted that optimum use of an agricultural region in technological terms depends partly upon the population to be supported, partly upon the economic system through which products are distributed, and partly upon the tastes, preferences, and needs of consumers that help to determine which crops are most productive. The all-important precondition for technological advance lies in a population's perception of the opportunities available in the region and in inter-regional intercourse.

The technological level of a community may be evaluated through the collection of data on tools used and skills practiced in the region. These may be classified according to the following categories:

(1) Agricultural technology: soil and water management, control of plant and animal genetics, pest control, and processing, storing, and marketing agricultural produce.

(2) Energy technology: the use of draught animals, fossil fuels, organic nonfossil fuels, hydraulic energy, electrical energy, solar, wind, geothermal and nuclear energy, and assorted minor energy sources. In many respects energy technology is a particularly critical area with respect to regional demographic carrying capacities, since if abundant, cheap energy becomes widely available, foods may be synthesized from inorganic or non-food organic matter, and ocean water may be freely distilled to the benefit of mankind. So it is that the United Nations and many independent countries are fostering research in the field of energy technology.

(3) Metallurgy: ferrous, ferroalloy, base-metal and light-metal production, and production of other of metals.

(4) Chemical technology: production of industrial chemicals, arti-

11

ficial fertilizers, acids, bases, alcohols, industrial gases, organic and pharmaceutical chemicals, glass, plastics, synthetics, and others.

(5) Manufacturing and process technology: food processing, textile making, production of machinery, transportation equipment, consumer durable and non-durable goods, handicrafts, and others.

(6) Technology of transportation by sea, land, and air: the development of port, terminal, and depot facilities, freight-handling equipment, and specialized storage and warehousing equipment.

(7) Health and medical technology: training of physicians, dentists, nurses, and technicians; providing hospital and medical school facilities and equipment and public health facilities such as plants for water purification and supply, sewage treatment, and public sanitation. This technological category has an immediate and profound effect on population change, since public health measures foster infant survival, which sometimes leads to rapid population increase.

(8) Time trends in technology: the rate of obsolescence of technological installations and techniques.

A very useful means for evaluating the state of technological development in a society makes use of the interrelationships among all of these categories as they are embodied in industries and occupations. Wassily Leontief[3] has devised a type of statistical table called an *Input-Output Table,* which analyzes the financial transactions of all of the industries in an economy in terms of the purchases of goods or services by each industry from all of the others, and the sales of each industry to all of the others. He shows that the economic structure of the Input-Output Table is directly related to the level and state of technological development of the region under study.[4]

Organization

In countless communities, a population employs technology and the resources of its environment through its distinctive organization to modify or, in some cases, to change completely that environment. Thus environmental determinism is the exception, rather than the rule. The collection of information about the organization of a society may be conveniently classified under some such schema as the following:

(1) Governmental organization: sources of political authority; mechanisms for the exercise of authority; limitations on authority:

the law; individual rights, privileges, prerogatives and duties; and governmental relationships with other political entities.

(2) Social organization: culture and its transmission, education; kinds and nature of subgroups within society; social differentiation of individuals: the roles played by men, women, children, families, class and caste members, members of religious groups, and so forth.

(3) Economic organization: the ownership of capital and land; the availability and organization of labor; the nature of economic incentives and goals; money; credit and banking systems; patterns of organization in the production and distribution of goods, services, and incomes; the nature and extent of domestic and foreign markets, including the status of the nation with respect to foreign exchange.

(4) Trends for change in the social, political, and economic organization of the region.

Social Psychology

This dimension is perhaps more elusive and difficult to approach than any of the others. It deals not only with the objective behavior, prejudices, and traditions of the regional populace, but also with subjective perceptions of the natural and interpersonal environment. Much social psychology is implicit in literature, language, humor, and folkways. Kevin Lynch[5] has convincingly shown that such perceptions, colored by the emotions attaching to cultural symbols, may not accord with objective reality, the consequent actions and decisions seeming incomprehensible or downright irrational to the individual equipped with a different set of perceptions. The plan that seems so practical to the demographer seeking to control population may completely contradict an individual's wishes in a culture where children are perceived as a guarantee of immortality; each's view seems suicidal to the other.

Accordingly, the following categories may be suggested for evaluating the prevailing social psychology of a given region:

(1) The relationship of the individual to the world: myths, value systems, mores, customs, and goals identified as presenting the consensus of the philosophical, religious, and traditional orientation of the people—attitudes towards change especially.

(2) Personal disorganization, its nature and extent: what is considered crime and antisocial activity; areas of adjustment; problems experienced by migrants elsewhere.

(3) Intergroup relationships: attitudes towards others; class, caste, ethnic, and national prejudices.

(4) Communications characteristics: public opinion as expressed in the mass media; the utilization of means of private communica-

tion; the number and intensity of choices and alternatives offered by the media; prevailing symbols used in the media.

If changes are to be effected in the technology, organization, and environment of a region—and hence its carrying capacity—either to increase the population or to improve the level of life, or both, the population must be psychologically willing to accept the changes, lest disorganization ensue which may defeat the effort. They must perceive the changed region and their part in it as a desirable goal.

Concluding Comments

Viewed in the light of the factors that combine to support a population at a given level in a given environment, any simple deterministic scheme that expresses well-being in terms of only one explanatory cause is probably more calculated to mislead than inform—be it the Malthusian over-simplification that makes population a function of the food-supplying capacity of the environment or any other form of environmental determinism, or indeed ideological determinism of an economic kind, whether Marxian or laissez-faire.

The classroom teacher, in approaching this broader perspective of demography with his students, may very well want to use regional analysis, especially that of the local community. In the manual by Hertzberg,[6] modes of demographic fact gathering, analyzing, and projecting are discussed in detail, and a plan is set forth whereby a teacher may guide his class in working up a description of the population of his community. Building upon that base, he may set students the tasks of gathering data under the categories of organization, technology, social psychology, and environmental change in their local area to relate to the projected demographic changes that they have already catalogued. Needless to say, for any one small and restricted community, all of the numerous subcategories detailed in the framework of the preceding section will not be significantly present, but some of them are sure to be, and while the teacher should not expect the analysis to be carried forward in all of the quantitatively sophisticated detail of the professional researcher, still the authors have found in their own work that when students have their attention drawn to the relevance of this kind of study to their ultimate well-being and the well-being of their community, they often develop very imaginative and worthwhile views of the changes in which they and their families are so inextricably involved.

It should be clear by now that the true end to be desired is much less the memorization or learning of facts or generalizations than it is the acquisition of an analytical and critical habit of mind. This is why we suggest a limited number of studies in depth. The students may better extend their intellectual powers in seeking out interrelationships among the facets of community life that explain demographic change than in being presented with sweeping generalizations that apply over continents or nations.

To this purpose, we have prepared the three sample studies which follow, believing them to be representative, not of the level of synthesis of the professional regional analyst, but rather of the level of synthesis which a well led secondary school class in geography might have within its powers to achieve.

CASE I: THE M'ZAB

The M'zab provides the interesting case of an extremely hostile environment, offering few useable resources but mastered through the efforts of a homogeneous population possessing a high order of technological skill and social organization.

Environment

The Mediterranean coast of Algeria slopes upward in a southerly direction for some two hundred miles. On these relatively well watered foothills is located the population core of Algeria. The Atlas Mountain system to the south is a broken, increasingly arid barrier region. The slopes to the south are barren dry limestone, dipping into the Sahara. On these limestone plateaus is to be found the M'zab, with its chief city, Ghardaia.

Seven settlements are found here, at altitudes ranging from 1900 to 2300 feet, in the middle of stony desert (*hamada*) crossed by eroded ravines (*wadis*). The only vegetation and animal life to be found in this setting is at the *wadi* bottoms. The general soil type is a well stratified, hard lime pedocal with embedded pieces of quartzy rock. The lime overlays marl in various places, and groundwater is to be found at the subterranean interface at depths of from 26 to 180 feet.

Weather and climate records do not exist for Ghardaia. At Touggourt to the northeast, the situation is roughly similar (see Table II-1), although the elevation is lower (226 feet). There is an average annual temperature of 72°F, with an absolute maximum of 122°F and an absolute minimum of 26°F. The average annual rainfall is only 2.9 inches, and the cloud cover averages less than 1/10. While air temperatures as high as 122°F have been recorded, ground temperatures have been measured up to 720°F. Dust storms are common, and the area is part of the source region for the desiccating *harmattan* (northeast wind).

Table II-1

MONTH	MEAN TEMPERATURE (in °F)	PRECIPITATION (in inches)
January	50*	.2
February	55	.4
March	61	.6**
April	69	.1
May	77	.2
June	89	.1
July	92**	.0
August	90	.0*
September	84	.0
October	72	.2
November	60	.6**
December	52	.4

* Minimum month.
** Maximum months.

Hot as is the day in midsummer, the night is often cool, 30 degrees cooler than the day, on the average. The rare water exposed to this furnacelike environment evaporates rapidly into the dry air, except where it can sink below the insulating surface of a *wadi*.

Water is at a premium, and the seven towns are laid out according to its availability, near *wadi* bottoms. Nevertheless, despite the forbidding environment, which provides little in the way of useful fauna or flora except a certain kind of scrub brush utilized for fuel, the following kinds of crops have been imported and flourish there: figs, oil palms, pomegranates, apricots, peaches, barley, beans, carrots, radishes, red pimento, rape, melons, tomatoes, rye, and wheat. Introduced domesticated animals include camels, sheep, and goats.

Population

Demographic data are grossly incomplete for the M'zab. The Mozabites are descended from a group of Berbers who began to emigrate from the Algerian coast inland around 900 A.D. Of the seven towns, El Ateuf, the oldest, was founded in 1013 A.D., Bu Nura and Beni Isguen in 1048 A.D., and Ghardaia, the most recent, in 1053 A.D. The other settlements were established at intermediate times.

Shortly after the French asserted control over the area in the 1880's, a census was made (see Table II-2).

Table II-2

TOWN	POPULATION	CAMELS	SHEEP	GOATS	PALM TREES
Ghardaia	8314	209	1000	507	60,591
Melika	2017	32	522	381	4032
Beni Isguen	5205	41	0	706	26,084
Bu Nura	1010	14	0	164	9600
El Ateuf	2346	10	0	1	17,476
Gerrara	3322	118	540	743	25,700
Berrain	3040	66	3670	1335	25,775
TOTALS:	25,252	490	5732	3837	166,261

From 1933 there are a few figures available. Ghardaia then had 12,000 inhabitants, with a count of 64,000 palm trees, and Berrain had 3000 inhabitants and 35,000 palm trees, and the total estimated population for the whole area was 30,000 with in excess of 150,000 palms. These data, though grossly incomplete, nevertheless suggest a static, stable society—a society in demographic equilibrium.

Technology

The fundamental technological problem for the Mozabites is the efficient utilization of groundwater. This has been attacked from the standpoint of hydraulic works construction and from the standpoint of minimum evaporation agriculture.

Some 3300 wells, dug originally with hand-wrought metal tools, supply the seven cities and their suburban gardens with water. The wells are too deep for the level devices used elsewhere in North Africa, even for the wheel and axle. The well orifice is therefore located on a low-gradient mound and the well itself lined with stone for the upper few yards and surmounted by a masonry yoke, on which a pulley is mounted. Water is drawn up by means of the pulley at the well mouth by a donkey or a camel walking downslope and is then transported to the irrigation ditches by means of leather bags. The irrigation ditch itself is lined with mortar, and a cover of cut limestone minimizes evaporation. When the water does not flow directly to an irrigated garden, it flows into a major irrigation leader. Many of these leaders converge in the garden districts, running like streets between the walled gardens;

in fact, they are often used as streets. At the time of irrigation (usually at night, to minimize evaporation), small sluices at the base of the garden walls are opened to admit the water through baffles that reduce the current.

From where the groundwater supply lies, upslope from the town, *qanats* (underground water galleries) connect the irrigation leaders with restraining dams, some quite large, carefully built and maintained in the highlands above the M'zab in readiness to impound the water from the cloudbursts that occasionally, though infrequently, occur.

The building materials commonly used in the M'zab, for dwellings as well as for irrigation works, are cut stone and *timshent,* a mortar obtained by burning lime with gypsum, using *wadi* scrub as a fuel. The only wood available for construction comes from the thinning out of palm trees when they are past the maximum bearing age. In order to conserve this resource, bent palms are used as forms, around which *timshent* is set. The palm core is then withdrawn, leaving a hollow column or arch for the typical central court of the Mozabite house. Wood is conserved, and the resulting hollow construction is superb insulation.

The agricultural technology is very ingenious. The camels, goats, and sheep grazing on *wadi* scrub are, of course, converters of waste grass into fiber, meat, milk, and manure. The manures are collected for use in the garden, along with human wastes. In addition, the lime and salts available in the surrounding desert are used as soil conditioners. Thus the Mozabite garden soil (like that cultivated by the Amish in Pennsylvania) improves with the years.

A multilevel, intercrop planting scheme retards evaporation and provides shade for sensitive plants. The palms tower over all, partly shading the fruit trees below. The lower bean bushes, in turn, benefit from the shade of the fruit trees, and at the lowest level, in the most shelter, are the ground crops. These tiered levels of shade keep soil temperatures low enough so that nitrogen compounds do not deteriorate, and transpiration modifies the climate within the garden into a pleasant one, even in intense summer.

The literature on manufacturing is very sketchy, but rug and textile spinning, dyeing, and weaving based partly on imported wool are practised at the handicraft level by Mozabite women.

Since 1934, Ghardaia has been linked with Algiers by an excellent all-weather road, and is, in fact, a junction of some importance. It is near Hassi R'Mel, the originating point of an important natural gas line terminating in Oran and Algiers, and 150 miles to the east is the main oil pipeline between Ohanet and Bougie.

18

Social Organization

Basic to the Mozabite society is the fact that they are a Moslem sect who approach the teachings of Mohammed in a literal and fundamentalist way, with a puritanical aspect to their beliefs and behavior that sets them apart from other North Africans. It was this that exposed them to the hostile actions of neighboring Moslems, driving them from the coast in a quest for security, which led them to attempt to colonize the forbidding region of the M'zab. At least until 1958 sentiments against other Moslems ran high in the seven towns, while Jews enjoyed toleration within the walls of Ghardaia, and Christians were allowed to live adjacent to, but outside, the walls.

Strength of religious feeling varies among the seven towns, with Ghardaia being the most liberal, and Beni Isguen, where all strangers are excluded from the city and gardens, the most intolerant. In all of the towns, non-residents are expected to be outside the walls by 6:00 P.M.

The extended family ruled by a patriarch is the rule, and land ownership, well ownership, and wealth is vested in the family. The owners sell the use of their wells to cultivators by the hour and accept the responsibility for maintaining the wells. The family lives on the produce of its gardens, together with supplementary meat and dairy products purchased in the town market. During the cool winter months, families live in town houses, but during the hot summer the town becomes deserted as the populace takes up residence in houses built in the gardens, taking advantage of the environment they have created. Not only is there a seasonal rhythm of migration, but a longer-term one as well.

Since meat, metal products, and other goods must be imported into the M'zab to elevate the living standard to a comfortable one, a measure of "foreign exchange," so to speak, must be earned. The Mozabites have no products worthy of export, so they export commercial skill. As a child, the male Mozabite lives in the M'zab, but at maturity he emigrates to the urban centers on the Algerian coast to earn wealth as a tradesman. Mozabite families run businesses as grocers, coal sellers, butchers, and general merchants in Oran, Algiers, and Constantine. As youths from a family go to the coast to establish themselves in the family businesses, their elders return to the M'zab with their earnings, to retire to the way of life of their ancestors.

Thus emigration has become institutionalized in law and custom. Loss of caste accompanies a refusal to emigrate, and returned men of wealth are selected as political leaders, thereby benefitting not only themselves, but their extended families. The returning successful merchants also run Mozabite commercial establishments which maintain contact with the coastal emigrés. In 1898 currency, the purchase volume of one of these merchants per year in Algiers amounted to $20,000—a substantial sum.

Within the Mozabite towns, all goods are transferred and sold at regular public auctions at which all residents have an equal right to bid. This laissez-faire, free-market type of economic organization is reputedly combined with political democracy, but detailed data are lacking on the municipal political organizations, so that the accuracy of that judgment may be doubted.

Women are married between the ages of nine to twelve to men averaging ten years their seniors. Since the men of that age spend substantial lengths of time away from home, the birth rate is held down, and women are rigorously confined to the home. Here, in her husband's absence, her authority over her children is absolute, enforced by the family elders. She is responsible for transmitting the culture and choosing partners for her children. Thus, it is the custom to educate women among the Mozabites, to facilitate the performance of their important social role.

Social Psychology

Although explicit information on this subject is absent from the literature, we gain at least the impression that the individual Mozabite of the equilibrium period had his world defined by his intense attachment to the soil, wells, and gardens of his forbears, and by his brief interlude as a stranger and visitor to the coast. Women, on the other hand, were, in general, denied even this latter perspective of a wider world. In terms of the strictly religious attitudes of the society, their tradition of persecution and refuge, and the closed nature of their society, we may suppose that the resistance to change on the part of the community leaders might be formidable.

Social disorganization, crime, and vice is not treated in the literature, so presumably it is not notably more common in the M'zab than elsewhere, but if this closed society were opened by changes and innovations, one might suspect that many problems of adjustment from an isolated, closed, religious community to an open, secular one would occur—restless discontent on the part of the young, and fearful traditionalism on the part of their elders.

Transportation and communication links are indeed increasingly joining the M'zab to the growing oil field communities with their young, predominately male, and comparatively wealthy populations, many of completely foreign culture. The input flow of information (via radio and the secular press) and of goods and services presents the Mozabites with a rapidly proliferating range of choices and alternatives. We may ask whether Mozabites will still tend to localize their business activities close to home, rather than far afield, and what implications changes might have for birth rates, child-raising practices, and family structure. Other questions suggest themselves. In view of the Mozabites' economic skills, on the one hand, and sets of prejudices, on the other, what kinds of reactions might be expected to the "invasion" of non-Mozabite population in the region?

As the range of choices increases for Mozabite young people while the fabric of their local community changes, what is the likelihood that emigration to the great cities of Algeria will occur? Finally, if small communities like those of the M'zab have increasing birth rates, yet the young people emigrate to the cities, where is the population upsurge most likely to be perceived? If the population upsurge of a nation is perceived in the urban centers, yet created in the villages, and if effective communications between the two regions is limited, what implications does this have for the demographer who wishes to promote the development of an effective national population policy?

Concluding Comments

The truly formidable, delicately balanced technological and social structure of this community has enabled it to prosper in the desert. All threads of organization return to the insurance of a supply of water and its conservation, and the securing of an economic beachhead on the coast for the enrichment of life. The Mozabite way of life survived a threat in the 1930's when Ghardaia became a road junction: enough Mozabite families remained in Algiers to locate a Mozabite rite mosque there. Now that the Sahara around Ghardaia is humming with natural gas and oil discoveries, what will be the effects on the delicate ecological balance of the M'zab? On the fact that the Algerian government is now Arab rather than French? Is the possibility of a collective Socialist government a real threat to the M'zab?

Frequently more questions are raised than answered by an ecological enquiry.

Data Limitations in the Literature

The demographic data on the M'zab is extremely sketchy and undetailed. Many gaps exist in the data on governmental structure, culture, and social change mechanisms. Economic circulation, on the other hand, is fairly well treated, as is energy, hydraulic, and agricultural technology. Metallurgy is apparently absent. Some chemical technology can be inferred from the making of *timshent*, fertilizer, and textile dyes. There is no data available on health and medical technology.

CASE II: THE IRISH FAMINE, 1845–1847

The potato, an introduced plant in the Irish ecology to begin with, became the mainstay of a monocultural subsistence agriculture. A blight invasion in 1845 brought disaster, which was compounded by maladjustments of technology and social organization to the environment, and which precipitated a population problem which has persisted until today.

Environment

Ireland is an island west of Great Britain that has been compared to a saucer; there is an elevated rim of low mountains, and a low central region of rolling relief and varied topography. The western highlands are structurally related to the Fenno-Scandic uplands, and they represent the emergence of a granitic basement complex above the later sedimentaries which overlie it in central Ireland. The entire island has been strongly glaciated, and so rock basin lakes and bogs, as well as other glacial features as drumlins, eskers, and moraines, are well known. The soils arising from this environment of decomposing granite and bog are generally acid and friable, and often deep.

Table II-3

MONTH	MEAN TEMPERATURE (in °F)	PRECIPITATION (in inches)
January	41*	2.7
February	41	2.2
March	43	2.0
April	46	1.9*
May	51	2.3
June	56	2.0
July	59	2.8
August	59**	3.0**
September	55	2.8
October	50	2.7
November	44	2.7
December	41	2.6

* Minimum month.
** Maximum month.

Ireland's climate is cool and moist (see Table II-3). At Dublin (elevation, 155 feet), near the Irish east coast, the average annual temperature is 49°F, with a range of only 19°F, and the average annual precipitation is 29.7 inches of rainfall. Cloud cover is the rule, and this factor together with Ireland's poleward location restricts evaporation, so that 29.7 inches of moisture is ample for agriculture.

From Dublin westward, precipitation and fog increase, due to the prevailing westerlies, which bear moisture from the Atlantic to the Irish western highlands. Nevertheless, the ocean modifies the temperature range, so that the absolute minimum (at Valentia) is 20°F, while the absolute maximum is 81°F. This is an absolute minimum temperature not much different from that of the M'zab, at a latitude analogous to that of Newfoundland-Labrador.

The potato itself was an introduced plant, having originated in the Western Hemisphere, which for a variety of social and environmental reasons had come to dominate Irish subsistence agriculture by the 1840's. Among the environmental reasons for the potato's success were the availability of deep, friable, acid soils and former grassland for potato cultivation; heavy rain and brisk, moist winds in the potato's growing season; the presence of high atmospheric humidity; and the absence of ecological enemies. While the farming potential delines from east to west in Ireland, the potato was ubiquitous: the sole crop in parts of the west, and the subsistence crop among cash crops in the east.

By 1845, an ecological enemy of the potato had invaded Ireland. The fungus *Phytophthora Infestans,* after having ravaged the North American potato crop, appeared in Ireland, having probably been carried across the Atlantic by ship. The disease organism was sensitive to heat and dryness and so adapted well to its new home. The crop of 1845 was the first Irish crop to fail, although crop failures had already occurred and famine ensued in North America and in Germany. Even stored potatoes were attacked, the organism being able to live upon the tubers as well as upon the rest of the plant.

After the failure of the 1846 crop, a climatic accident contributed to the distress. In the winter of 1846–1847, the moderating westerlies failed, and air masses from Scandinavia and Russia invaded Ireland. Cold, snow, and freezing of water bodies were the results. It will be shown that the typhus epidemic of 1847 was directly linked to this severe winter.

Population

Estimates of Ireland's population in 1841 range from 6 million to 8 million. We may accept the conservative figure at 6,529,000. The famine

23

and the accompanying emigration reduced the population by an estimated 2 million persons, of whom 1 million probably died, and 1 million emigrated. Those who found resources, strength, and courage to emigrate were often people in the vigorous prime of life, leaving behind a destitute and aging population.

One hundred years later, Ireland's population was 2,961,000 (1951), and it was an aging population. We find northwest Ireland in 1951 with as many people aged 70 as aged 30. The population loss in Ireland during the famine decade (1841–1851) has been calculated as follows.

Province	Per Cent Loss
Leinster (E.)	15.5
Ulster (N.)	16.0
Munster (S.)	23.5
Connaught (W.)	28.5

Clearly in the south and west, where dependence on the potato was all but absolute, the losses were greatest. The famine years form a kind of demographic watershed in Ireland. Population growth before this period resembles that of the rest of Europe. Following this period, despite periodic surges, the overall effect has been decline.

Technology

Prior to 1840, Ireland was technologically backward. Not only were there no significant industries for local or export markets, but commerce lagged as well. Peat was the only extensive fuel resource, and was used for domestic heating almost exclusively. Except for occasional estates where cash crops were raised for export, agricultural technology had hardly risen beyond a neolithic level in many remote rural areas. Indeed, especially in the west, where turf cottages and hoe agriculture predominated, where illiteracy was the rule, and where the vast majority of the inhabitants lived almost completely outside of European technology, much could have undoubtedly been learned from the more technologically advanced American Indian cultures.

Medical technology in Ireland was utterly unprepared for the famine disaster. In 1841 there were only 39 infirmaries for general patients in all of Ireland, mostly in urban areas. For example the ratio was 1 infirmary to 6000 persons in Dublin, but 1 infirmary to 366,000 persons in Mayo (in the west). The utter lack of sanitary facilities for waste disposal in the cities made effective measures against the typhus epidemic of 1847 impossible.

But the inadequacies of technology extended beyond the boundaries of Ireland. The international scientific community itself was inadequate to the task of dealing with the blight, even though the means for check-ing it (a mixture of copper sulfate and quicklime called Bordeaux mix-ture) would have been easily available, had it been known. Nor did the early North American potato failures and the German failure give rise to intensive research. There was an inadequacy of scientific com-munication and coordination of findings. In 1845, Rev. M. J. Berkeley, after studying the blight, reported the association of leaf fungus with all cases of blight and suggested the fungus as the cause. The scientific community, committed to a doctrine that fungus was inevitably the *result* of decay, and not the cause, rejected the suggestion. Only in the 1860's then was the causal role of the fungus proved, and in 1885, the Bordeaux treatment applied.

Technology failed even in famine relief. Maize was imported from the United States as an emergency measure. Millers in Ireland ground it in the same fashion that wheat is ground, making an irritating, rough, and indigestible flour which caused serious illness in the famine-weakened people who used it.

Social Organization

Traditionally, Irish society has been organized around the clan: an extended-family aggregation claiming a common ancestor. Within the ancient clan there were three horizontal classes, the chief and his family, the free tenant fighters (kerns), and the workers of the land. Property ownership was vested in the clan, rather than in the individual.

During the Elizabethan conquest of Ireland, the clan leaders either fled, or capitulated and intermarried with their conquerors. Thus, effec-tive control of Ireland passed into the hands of an Anglo-Irish aristoc-racy. During this period, the economy began to develop. The export trade from Galway, Cork, Waterford, and Drogheda included timber, wool, linen and woolen yarn, skins, meat, and live cattle. Dublin im-ported metals, luxuries, and wines. The cities were developing com-mercial centers but were still islands of cash economy in a precommercial ocean.

The potato by 1623 had become a staple in the countryside and by 1660 was the basic food in Ireland. The spread of this crop was facili-tated by the fact that Ireland had been a pastoral country. In England, the established practices surrounding the three-field system had impeded the acceptance of a new crop.

In the 17th century, the period of Cromwell brought disaster to Ireland. The force with which the Irish uprising against Cromwell was crushed had the effect of rigorously separating the Catholic majority from the Protestant minority. The infant commercial establishment was

25

smashed, as all non-agricultural activity was denied to Catholics. A caste system was the result, along with the denial of social mobility to the majority. The clan holdings were transferred to loyal Protestant English vassals, and with the chiefs fled or capitulated and the kerns merged with the cultivators, the clan system degenerated.

Institutionalizing and summarizing these developments were the penal laws, instituted in 1695 and remaining in effect until 1829, only 16 years before the famine. These laws barred Catholics from the army, navy, law, commerce, all civic activities, from the purchase of land, from attending or maintaining any school at home or abroad, in fact, and from participating in anything but subsistence agriculture. The year 1845 found most Irish agriculturalists, especially in the West, completely outside the money economy.

At the time of the famine, political decision-making was vested in the English Parliament, by the Act of Union of 1801. Throughout most of the famine years, this body was dominated by a group of men who were, however philanthropically oriented, dominated by a dedication to the principles of *laissez-faire* economics of the most doctrinaire sort.

Thus, while there was food in Ireland, it was the position of the English government that the operation of a free economy would permit the poor to purchase food, if the prices could be kept down. Accordingly, for a long time English policy was directed towards controlling prices. This policy completely overlooked the indigent masses outside of the cash economy who flocked to urban centers seeking relief. Grain was therefore actually exported from Ireland in the famine years in the absence of purchasing power to buy it.

There were fewer legal limitations to mortgage requirements in Ireland than in England prior to the famine. Consequently, heavy debt was the rule among the large holders of Irish land. The landholders were required by Irish Law to maintain workhouses for relief: no "outdoors" relief (the equivalent of home relief today) was permitted, as it was under the English law. The heavily mortgaged landlords were thus legally required to support the indigent from their districts in workhouses, an impossible task in general famine conditions. Rather than face personal bankruptcy, the landlord evicted his tenants, thus claiming that they were not district residents. Faced by starvation and eviction, the more prosperous tenants chose emigration. Those who had to remain were caught in a socio-economic doomsday machine.

Outdoor relief, authorized in the winter of 1846, was only on the condition of working on public works. Those still strong enough to work had to expose themselves, in the garments which remained after pawning their wardrobes for food, to an unusually terrible winter. When typhus appeared in 1847, the epidemic culminated an ecological chain which can be described as follows:

1. The potato failure led to famine.
2. Famine led to indigence and the selling of property for food.
3. The socio-political structure drove people to urban centers.
4. Outdoor winter work relief in the towns led to further weakness and illness.
5. The ragged, weakened people in the urban centers huddled together for warmth.
6. As they huddled together, lice spread through their rags, carrying typhus.

Additional thousands of refugees fled Ireland during 1847 to avoid typhus and famine. They poured into North America and England. Many ships found a backhaul of refugees, however little they paid for passage, more lucrative than ballast, and so ripples from the disaster in Ireland washed into Canadian, Boston, New York, and Liverpool slums.

The English government, dedicated to *laissez-faire* to the end, refused to provide seed potatoes to the survivors after the famine years on economic grounds. Thus, mass emigration probably continued longer than ecologically necessary.

Social Psychology

In the Irish case, the ruling class identified with the outlook and perspectives of the English squire. Since they were, by choice, urban dwellers, frequently living abroad, the west country Irish peasant was outside of their realm of perception. From this stemmed illusions such as the naive assumption that most Irish families were within the cash economy, and that fiscal policies might alleviate the disaster.

The inflexible adherence to preconceived ideology was not limited to the governing classes, however. Scientists committed to a specific theory of fungus propagation rejected a hypothesis which would have proven correct regarding the cause of the blight, eschewing the possibility of empirical testing in favor of a test by dogma.

On the other hand, the world view of the Irish peasant had been rigidly constricted and circumscribed by generations of policy directed towards limiting his access to media of communication and circumscribing his arena of choice, so that although he was caught in the maelstrom of the disaster, he lacked the facilities for fully communicating his plight to the government whose views were formed behind the filtered lenses of their faulty perceptions.

The incidence of crime and all other forms of social disorganization quickly multiplied, occasioning ill-thought-out stopgap remedies that did nothing to prevent the demoralization of the populace and the break-down even of family structure. Compounding the crisis was the prejudice and mutual hostility on an intergroup basis between the Irish Catholic peasantry and the Anglo-Irish rulers. To alleviate the famine would have required the whole-hearted, compassionate mutual cooperation of these two groups. This was impossible in the social context of nineteenth-century Ireland. The contemporary world abounds with examples of societies where the population is split between a colonial ruling minority and a peasant majority, where such a split has recently prevailed, or where two or more mutually hostile groups occupy the same region. Environmental crises in these cases often trigger internicine hostilities or disorganization leading to death, pestilence, or flight, instead of an organized confrontation of the problem. Students might well enjoy discussing these problems.

Demographically, the effect on Ireland was especially to decimate the younger population and to send thousands of persons of childbearing age out of the country. The resulting population was not only smaller but older and less fertile. The poverty, lack of opportunity, and demoralization led to the acceptance of the custom of late marriage in the populace. Accordingly, the Irish population approached a new equilibrium at about half the pre-famine number.

Concluding Comments

The ecological tragedy in Ireland was compounded and multiplied by the acts of decision-makers who chose, in the light of widely accepted ideologies, to follow policies which aggravated, rather than alleviated, the catastrophe, in the ironic conviction that they were governing wisely. Faith in an abstract body of dogma rather than in empirically based studies of the real ecological situation forfeited the lives of many in the afflicted population.

In the case of the Mozabites, a hostile environment was mastered by focusing technology and social organization on it, through a determined population. In the Irish case, technology was not brought to bear on Irish problems until too late, and the organization of the society involved was utterly inadequate to its task. The Mozabite population was united and culturally homogenous; the Irish population was internally divided and culturally at war.

We might ask what policies the leadership might have followed to more helpfully deal with the disaster, and might try to anticipate the response of various political bodies today to a similar event. In what respects, for example, does the current (in 1968) Biafran-Nigerian crisis resemble what happened in Ireland?

Data Limitations in the Literature

Outside of serious and probably irremedial gaps in demographic and statistical data on nineteenth-century Ireland, there is an abundance of material on the other categories of information. Bias and strong emotion are common in the literature, however, and care must be exercised to separate analysis from accusation.

CASE III: MORRISVILLE, PENNSYLVANIA

In 1950, Morrisville, in Bucks County, Pennsylvania, was a rural community outlying Trenton and Philadelphia. Dairying and truck farming, the bases of the local economy, linked Morrisville to the adjacent urban markets. Changes in the technology of steel production in a locale more than a thousand miles away from Morrisville as well as discoveries in the tropics converged to readjust the organization of the steel industry, bringing the Fairless works of United States Steel to Morrisville and effecting great changes in the community.

Environment

Morrisville, Pennsylvania is located near the head of the tidewater zone of the Delaware River, where the natural channel is still 14 feet deep. To the northwest the Piedmont rises, and to the southeast the coastal plain extends. Trenton is across the river, and Philadelphia is downstream on the same bank, about 20 miles away. The easy access from New York City through Trenton to Philadelphia, in terms of the flat land and the direct route, has led to intensive canal, railroad, and highway development (in that order). Thus Morrisville is well served by transportation channels.

The climate is admirable for mid-latitude dairying. The records for nearby Harrisburg, Pennsylvania, at an altitude of 361 feet, are shown in Table II-4.

The yearly average temperature is 52°F, and the range is 45°F, with a yearly average precipitation of 37.2 inches. There is a long growing season, with evenly distributed rainfall throughout. Irrigation is not usually required, and the ground is frozen only three months during the year. This permits soil infiltration most of the year. Enough fodder can be raised and stored to sustain dairy herds, and the winter is cool enough to restrict the insect pests that afflict cattle. By the same token, the Delaware never freezes over to the extent that the channel cannot be kept open. Water pollution and water supply is becoming a problem, however, as the burgeoning urban population between Baltimore and New York City turn their attention to the Delaware watershed.

Table II-4

MONTH	MEAN TEMPERATURE	PRECIPITATION (in inches)
January	30*	3.0
February	30	2.7
March	40	3.1
April	51	3.0
May	62	2.9
June	70	3.7
July	75**	3.5
August	73	4.1**
September	66	3.4
October	54	3.0
November	43	2.0*
December	33	2.9

* Minimum month.
** Maximum month.

The grey-brown forest soils in the vicinity are admirable for pasturage and mixed farming, and they also have good structural properties for building. On the site of the Fairless plant is a large area of marsh, which is advantageous to the steel mill.

Technology

Until quite recently, several technological factors favored an Appalachian or Great Lakes site for a steel mill, as opposed to an Atlantic Coastal Plain site. Before 1900, in the days of the beehive coke oven, much of the weight of a ton of coal was wasted. Thus, it was desirable to locate coke ovens and blast furnaces near coal deposits to avoid transporting what would ultimately be waste. When the byproduct coke oven was invented, all of this changed. No longer was there much waste in a ton of coal, so steel mills were established convenient to iron ore; on the Great Lakes, where Minnesota, through Duluth, was the great supplier.

Since the 1940's, the Minnesota ores have been partially exhausted, and new ore supplies have been discovered in Liberia and Venezuela. The eastern tidewater is an ideal place to take advantage of these ores. Furthermore, transportation costs of coal and iron ore are more than offset by advances in the technology of steelmaking. The L.-D. Basic Oxygen process saves $3 to $10 a ton in costs over the old Open Hearth. Thus a steel-making corporation can absorb the transportation expense for ore from Liberia and Venezuela and for coal from Appalachia.

Much more critical for today's steelmaking is water. The entire

American steel industry uses about 4 billion gallons a day. Even a plant that maximizes water conservation, like the desert plant at Fontana, California, requires 3 million gallons a day. Technology has made it possible for salt water and urban liquid wastes to be used as coolant, so it became possible to locate a plant on the Delaware tidewater.

The 3800-acre site includes two 1500-ton-capacity blast furnaces, a 1200-ton coke plant, a 30,000-kilowatt thermal electric plant, and a row of 3000-ton-capacity steel furnaces. The plant has a capacity of 2 million tons of steel per year, about equal to the entire steel capacity of Sweden. It went into operation in December 1952, but its operation was handicapped by the fact that the federal government had not yet appropriated funds for dredging the Delaware to a depth sufficient to accommodate the largest ore vessels. Thus, some ore had to be unloaded at Philadelphia into trains to feed the mill.

Social Organization

Opposition to the Morrisville plant mobilized around the issue of dredging the Delaware. While United States Steel and the manufacturers along the upper Delaware estuary exerted pressure to dredge the channel, a broader-based coalition of groups opposed it. New Jersey's opposition centered around Camden's claim that dredging the Delaware would open Camden's water supply to salt water intrusion. Great Lakes congressmen opposed it in revenge for eastern opposition to the St. Lawrence Seaway Project. Representatives Kirwan of Ohio and Walter of Pennsylvania mobilized opposition in the House of Representatives. Representative Kirwan's district was the locale of Youngstown Sheet and Tube Corporation, and Representative Walter's district was the locale of Bethlehem Steel. Youngstown Sheet and Tube and Bethlehem Steel were seeking to merge, and both were competitors of United States Steel.

To climax the problem, United States Steel had initially proposed to build only a rolling mill at Morrisville, but it had been persuaded by the Truman Administration, in the light of the Korean War, to build a fully integrated plant. In 1952, as the mill opened, General Eisenhower was elected President. The Eisenhower Administration, under the aim of promoting economy in government, opposed appropriating funds for the dredging and urged local financing. Since harbor and channel improvement has been a function of the Corps of Engineers for years, an impasse resulted. The channel was finally dredged when government policies changed after 1956.

The presence of the mill changed the organization of Bucks County, as satellite plants serving the Fairless Works grew up around Morris-

31

ville. The influx of employees sought housing, and land values rose as developments grew up. The community schools and service facilities were crowded and required expansion. Rising real estate taxes drove farmers to sell to developers, and the suburbanization cycle was in full swing. Facilities for retailing, wholesaling, and banking followed, and Morrisville and its environs, which in 1950 were rural, relating to a local region, have become urban, relating to a global region.

Population

Population and population density more than doubled in the ten years following 1950.

Table II-5

Population Change in Bucks County Township

	1950	1960
Population	144,620	308,567
Density*	236/square mile	500/square mile
Urban population	54,145	232,268

* The area of Bucks County is 617 square miles.

A county that had been 67 per cent rural became 75 per cent urban. The total population increased by 113.4 per cent, the urban population increased by 329.0 per cent, while the rural population decreased by 15.7 per cent.

In the immediate locality of Morrisville, the results were even more striking. Population increased in the region of Morrisville and the contiguous townships from 1940 to 1950 by about 80 per cent. From 1950 to 1960 it increased by 370 per cent. In 1960, in formerly rural Bucks County, the labor force is listed as 115,565 persons, of which 46,026, or about 39 per cent, are engaged in manufacturing and another 10 per cent are engaged in retailing. A real demographic revolution has occurred in Bucks County.

Table II-6

Population Change in the Vicinity of Morrisville

	BRISTOL	LOWER MAKEFIELD	FALLS TOWNSHIP (includes Morrisville)	MIDDLETOWN	TOTAL
1960	59,289	8604	29,082	26,894	113,869
1950	12,184	3211	3540	4987	23,922
1940	5857	1841	2364	3136	13,198

Social Psychology

The traditions, values, and prejudices of the residents in the region of Morrisville prior to 1950 were much more rural than urban in nature. Value was attached to being an old resident of the area rather than a newcomer, and stability was more highly regarded than change. Families had continuously occupied the same farms for several generations and had intermarried, forming an informal class of great influence in village and county affairs. It was typical for most residents to know each other personally. The individual saw himself as a member of a quiet circumscribed community of farming and small business people in a situation of long established stability.

This tightly organized, relatively closed system was subjected to the entry of 120,223 persons in the years from 1950 to 1960, a number virtually equal to the entire 1950 population. The new people were young, mobile, urban-oriented workers who had no deep environmental roots and who viewed themselves as ready to move wherever economic opportunity beckoned. With their entrance into Bucks County they brought a new way of life, oriented towards the communications media of the urban metropolis such as radio, television, and the cinema. Their influx led to the widening of the range of choices of the population, as the increasing density of population brought an increasing density of businesses offering novel lines of goods and services, while the earnings of the newcomers offered greater opportunity to county business people.

In the old resident's view, it was normal for the individual to work where he lived: on the farm or near his village store. It was also proper for the entire family, including—in some cases—more than one generation, to live near one another and share in one another's work. The family was viewed as a working as well as a domestic unit.

The newcomer, however, was habituated to a more specialized way of life. Only one conjugal family lived in a residence, and the workers in the family scattered daily by means of automobile and public transportation to their separate jobs, coming together for the evening meal, perhaps, and for weekend visits to the grandparents, but otherwise working and relaxing in the company of others—many of them strangers.

To the newcomers, the dedication of the old-timers to rural ways of life and their tactics to obstruct new programs in the now outgrown forms of local government seemed an unwarranted and thoughtless blocking of progress. For the old-timers it was a matter of preserving as much as possible the old values that they cherished as the legitimate values of life. The relations between the two groups became marred by a tacit mutual hostility.

The new environment, being unfamiliar, to a certain extent, to the

33

young people of both groups and building up rapidly in density, was now characterized by increasing rates of social disorganization. In such communities, as a general rule, indices of social disorganization, such as crime and mental illness rates, increase with residential density. Recent work has suggested that in urbanizing portions of the United States, 30,000 persons per square mile marks the critical point at which population density becomes insupportable and tends to diminish.[6] As Bucks County grows and becomes more integrated into the Philadelphia regional metropolitan system, will densities eventually move upwards to this level? What further changes might occur as the process of urbanization continues? What is likely to be the fate of the older population swallowed up in the change?

Concluding Comments

After 1950, Bucks County became transformed from a homogeneous farming region of limited extent to what the geographer terms "a nodal region of world-wide scope," influenced by environmental factors from as far away as Venezuela, through the communications channels of a potentially hostile Caribbean region. All of this came about through the introduction of a new technological-economic institution in the area, prompted by technological and environmental change in the Great Lakes region.

The more highly organized and widely organized the web of communities becomes, the less amenable does analysis seem via a simplistic biological-ecological model of the social Darwinian kind.

Limitations of Data

In this case abundant demographic and environmental data exists. Some specific technological data are regarded as "trade secrets" and are unavailable, as are some data on the political struggle over the dredging of the Lower Delaware.

BIBLIOGRAPHY

The three case studies were largely based upon material contained in the following publications.

Case I. The M'zab

Brunhes, Jean. *Human Geography*. Chicago: University of Chicago Press, 1920.
Kendrew, W. G. *Climates of the Continents*. New York: Oxford University Press, 1953.

Larford, Claude. "Ghardaia, austera guardiana del M'zab." *Revista Geografica Americana* (October 1934), pp. 259–268.

deLyee de Belleau, M. "Les femmes captives et gardiennes du M'zab." *La Nature* (January 1, 1937), pp. 26–32.

de Mazieres, Marc. "Une excursion dans le M'zab." *Revue de Geographie Marocaine.* Annee 20–21 (March 1937), pp. 411–423.

Raineau, Michel. "Le M'zab et ces curieux habitants." *Terre, Air, Mer.* (September-October 1933), pp. 168–174.

Suter, Karl. "Il problema idrico nelle oasi dello M'zab." *Bollettino della Societa Georgrafica Italiana.* Series VIII, II (1958), pp. 74–97.

Case II: The Irish Famine, 1845–1847

Cousens, S. H. "The Regional Pattern of Emigration During the Great Irish Famine, 1846–51." *Institute of British Geographers: Transactions and Papers,* 1960. Publications No. 28, 1960, pp. 119–134.

Douglas, J. N. H. "Irish Depopulation—Some of Its Associated Problems." *Don* (May 1962), pp. 20–24.

Freeman, T. W. *Ireland: Its Physical, Historical, Social, and Economic Geography.* London: Dutton, 1958.

Ryan, W. J. L. "Some Irish Population Problems." *Population Studies* IX: 2 (November 1955), pp. 185–188.

Salaman, Redcliffe. *The Influence of the Potato on the Course of Irish History.* Dublin, 1943. Pamphlet.

Woodham-Smith, C. *The Great Hunger.* New York: Harper and Row, 1963.

Case III: Morrisville, Pennsylvania

Alexander, J. W. *Economic Geography.* Englewood Cliffs, N. J.: Prentice-Hall, Inc., 1963.

Alexandersson, Gunnar. "Changes in the Location Pattern of the Anglo-American Steel Industry: 1948–1959," *Economic Geography* (April 1961), pp. 95–114.

"Big Steel Steps Up Expansion Program." *Business Week* (December 16, 1950), p. 20.

"Lighting Up the Fairless Works." *Business Week,* (December 20, 1952), p. 30.

"Steel: Capacity Outstrips Supply of Raw Materials." *Business Week* (September 22, 1951), pp. 22–24.

Peterman, Ivan H. "Delay on the Delaware," *Barron's* (March 12, 1956), p. 5.

Perham, John C. "Morrisville Mix," *Barron's* (October 26, 1953), p. 1. U.S. Census of Population and Housing, 1960.

Stone, Joseph K. "Oxygen in Steelmaking," *Scientific American,* 218 (April 1968), pp. 24–31.

U.S. Census of Population and Housing, 1960.

NOTES

[1] Hazel W. Hertzberg, *Teaching Population Dynamics.*

[2] Erich W. Zimmermann, *World Resources and Industries.* New York: Harper and Brothers, 1951.

[3] Leontief, *Input-Output Economics,* Oxford University Press, 1966, contains this material. See also Scientific American, *Technology and Economic Development* in the bibliography following in Chapter 3.

[4] The articles by Wassily Leontief are: "The Structure of the American Economy" and "The Structure of Development," which may be obtained from: W. H. Freeman and Company, *Scientific American Reprints,* 660 Market Street, San Francisco, California 94104.

[5] Kevin Lynch, *The Image of the City.* Cambridge, Mass.: M.I.T. Press, 1960.

[6] Hazel W. Hertzberg, *op. cit.*

[7] Bruce E. Newling, "Urban Growth and Spatial Structure: Mathematical Models and Empirical Evidence," *The Geographical Review* 56 (April 1966), pp. 213–225.

III. An Annotated Bibliography

The following bibliography attempts to provide teachers and their students with some basic materials useful for studying population in an ecological framework. It is impossible to cover all of the voluminous literature on this type of study; thus our list is a selective one. It includes only English-language works, and eliminates much literature which is overly technical or too narrow in scope. When a particular concept is considered basic and no general work is available, a technical work is, by necessity, included. We have tried to concentrate on recent and readily available literature in order to provide the reader with up-to-date and accessible materials. In some cases, if a work is old or difficult to obtain but is considered a classic and is unusually pertinent, it is included. The authors concentrate on presenting basic theoretical and general works, with a sampling of research aids and several sample case studies.

Ecological study is, by nature, interdisciplinary, so that the scope of the bibliography is broad, including works from the field of geography, demography, sociology, anthropology, economics, political science, as well as ecology. Since the material in these fields is vast, and since there are separate bibliographies available in each field, we usually cite only *examples* of particular materials, assuming that the teacher will fill in the gaps according to his needs and the needs of his students.

Unfortunately, there is little available at the reading level of high school students in this area, and only a limited number of works are written specifically for the teacher. Most publications are directed to a professional audience. Therefore, the teacher will have to adapt many of the readings for student use. The articles, books, or parts of books thought to be on a level suitable to secondary school students are marked with an **S.** The publications thought to be fundamental in nature, particularly useful, and extremely important to consider are noted with an asterisk (*).

The bibliography is divided into three principal sections, with subdivisions, as follows.

    I. Theoretical and General Introductory Works
        A. Theories of Ecology

37

  B. Ecological Variables and Their Interrelationships
  C. The Ecological Approach to Urban Regions
 II. General Aids
  A. Series
  B. Serials
  C. Statistical Sources
  D. Bibliographies
  E. Visual Aids and Methods
 III. Regional Case Studies
  A. Sample Case Bibliographies
  B. Collected Case Studies
  C. Individual Case Study Ideas

In Sections I and III, collected readings are noted separately. Specific articles within these anthologies, thought to be particularly noteworthy, are cited individually.

In organizing the material, it was found that several works contained material applicable to two or more areas and could be classified in two or more sections. These works are cross-listed, with a main entry in the section to which they are considered most pertinent.

In cases where free or inexpensive materials are available, the addresses of the publishers or distributors are noted. If a teacher finds a book particularly useful, he may order that work from the publishers, as noted in the citation. Many works are in paperback (marked with a **Pa**) and may be purchased at a relatively small cost.

Works that are inexpensively available in the Bobbs-Merrill reprint series (most of which cost $.25 each) are given the designation **B-M Reprint** followed by the catalog number. Works available as reprints from *Scientific American* ($.20 each) are given the designation **SA** followed by the identification number. The following addresses should be used in ordering.

The Bobbs-Merrill Company, Inc.
4300 West 62nd Street
Indianapolis, Indiana 46268

Scientific American Offprints
W. H. Freeman and Company
660 Market Street
San Francisco, California 94104

THEORETICAL AND GENERAL
INTRODUCTORY WORKS

This section is designed to provide literature primarily for the teacher on the theory, scope, nature, and content of ecology. Part A includes works of various theorists, presenting several different perspectives of ecological thought, including human ecology, cultural ecology, and urban ecology. The broader sense in which we view ecology, however, has not been dealt with to any great extent in the literature, so the few works which have our approach are marked with an asterisk. It is hoped that the material in this subsection will help provide the teacher with the concepts for looking at society through "ecological glasses."

As we have emphasized in the previous chapters, ecology requires interdisciplinary study. Scholars study one, several, or all of the ecological variables, depending on the nature of their fields and their approaches, and Part B of this section provides material on the five ecological factors and their interrelationships. These are general works, in the sense that they rarely refer to any particular community or region. They are highly varied in that they consider different factors and different interrelationships. Thus, we include works by demographers who consider the population factor in particular, and also works by population geographers, who emphasize primarily population *and* environmental variables. There are works by economists who emphasize the variables of technology and organization. One may also note selections by archeologists, anthropologists, sociologists, historians, and even urban planners. Many selections stress the role of one or two factors and consider the others only peripherally, or not at all. The annotations in Part B therefore note the particular viewpoint of the author and the factors he studies. Very few selections consider all five factors.

The last part in this section, Part C, is very similar to Part B, except that the writers consider the interrelationship of factors in urban regions and metropolitan areas. Here we list some background material for studying these regions, and cite those writers who look at city growth, structure, and distributions in an ecological perspective.

A. THEORIES OF ECOLOGY

1. Duncan, Otis Dudley. "Human Ecology and Population Studies." In Philip M. Hauser and Otis Dudley Duncan, eds. *The Study of Population: An Inventory and Appraisal.* Chicago: University of Chicago Press, 1959, pp. 678–710.

An up-to-date, comprehensive outline of the ecological study of population. Clear, concise statement concerning the interrelationship of factors in the "ecological complex" (pp. 681–684). Does not consider social psychology. Basic introduction to the field for secondary school teachers. Much of the technical, methodological, and theoretical material may be skimmed.

2. *Eyre, S. R. and G. R. J. Jones, eds. *Geography as Human Ecology; Methodology by Example.* New York: St. Martin's Press, 1966. 308 pp.

The eleven essays contained in this commendable anthology are excellent examples of regional case studies written in an ecological framework. Each essay considers the dynamic relationships among factors in an ecosystem, and to each is appended a bibliography which may lead teacher and student to necessary supplementary materials. Includes a forthright introductory essay by the editors, emphasizing human ecology as the central integrating theme for geography. Highly recommended source for model case studies.

3. Geertz, Clifford. *Agricultural Involution.* See No. 215.

4. *Gist, Noel P. and Sylvia Fleis Fava. *Urban Society,* 5th ed. New York: Thomas Y. Crowell Co., 1964. 623 pp.

An urban sociology college text, largely devoted to the ecological structure of cities, probably the best of its kind. Considers all five factors in the ecosystem and briefly demonstrates how they operate in the city. Reviews the important theory and content of urban ecology. Clear, well written introduction to urban ecology, highly recommended for the teacher. Excellent bibliography.

5. Hauser, Philip M. "Ecological Aspects of Urban Research." In Leonard White, ed. *The State of the Social Sciences.* Chicago: University of Chicago Press, 1956, pp. 229–254.

A survey of the development of ecological research on urban communities, tracing changes in theoretical orientation, and methods of research. Useful overview of urban ecology, with helpful bibliographical materials.

6. *Hawley, Amos H. *Human Ecology.* New York: Ronald Press, 1950. 456 pp.

This well written introduction to the study of population in an ecological framework has not been superseded. Part 2, "The Human Aggregate," provides the basic methodology for understanding the mechanics of population growth, composition, and distribution, suitable for students and teachers; see especially Chapter 6, "Habitat and Population." Part 3 is concerned with the fundamentals of spatial distribution, Chapters 13 and 14, "The Spatial Aspects of Ecological Organization," being most important. Part 4, an excellent outline of the phenomena of urban ecology, covers population growth and expansion. A clear, non-technical work, highly recommended for teachers, but with many passages appropriate for students.

7. McKenzie, Roderick D. "The Scope of Human Ecology." In George Theodorson, ed. *Studies in Human Ecology.* Evanston, Illinois: Row Peterson and Co., 1961, pp. 30–36.

An early interpretation of the major ecological processes, as determined by environmental, technological, social organizational, and cultural factors. A classic statement of ecology.

8. "Orienting Ecology to Theory and Application." *Social Forces,* 32: 317–375, May 1954.

An entire issue devoted to various aspects of human ecology, including theoretical and methodological research and case studies. The bibliographies cite articles of particular interest.

9. *Park, R. E., E. W. Burgess and R. D. McKenzie. *The City.* Chicago: University of Chicago Press, 1925. 228 p. **Pa**

A collection of essays representing the classical approach to human ecology, stressing natural competition and economics as the major influences on the spatial distribution of people and activities. See especially "The Growth of the City" by Ernest W. Burgess, in which he presents his concentric-ring urban growth theory, and "The Ecological Approach to the Study of the Human Community" by Roderick D. McKenzie. A fundamental work.

10. Park, Robert Ezra. *Human Communities.* Glencoe, Illinois: The Free Press, 1952. 262 pp.

A collection of essays outlining the basic concepts of human ecology, as derived from the study of plant and animal communities. Examines the effect of ecological processes upon the spatial distribution of cities and metropolitan communities.

11. Reissman, Leonard. "The Ecologists—Analysts of Urban Patterns." In Reissman, *The Urban Process.* London: Free Press of Glencoe, 1964, pp. 122–149.

An excellent survey of the growth and development of ecological theory as it applies to urban areas. Provides a clear-cut summary of the theories of urban growth by Burgess, Hoyt, and Harris and Ullman. Teachers and advanced **SHS**.

12. Steward, Julian H. *The Theory of Culture Change.* Urbana, Illinois: University of Illinois Press, 1955. 222 pp.

Somewhat technical for those without background in anthropology, but extremely worthwhile. "The Concept and Method of Cultural Ecology" provides an excellent summary of the anthropologist's view of ecology. Includes material on the Great Basin Shoshonean Indians, adaptable for case studies, and concerned with the inter-relationship of population, community organization, environment, and technology.

13. Schnore, Leo F. "Geography and Human Ecology." *Economic Geography,* 37:207–217, July 1961.

Includes passages explaining the nature of contemporary human ecology, the differences between ecology and geography, and the contact points between ecology and geography. A useful clarification of the interrelationship between the two fields. Teachers only.

14. *Theodorson, George A., ed. *Studies in Human Ecology.* Evanston, Illinois: Row Peterson and Co., 1961. 621 pp.

Probably the most comprehensive anthology of readings in human ecology, including significant theoretical articles and selected case studies. Each of five sections includes a thorough introductory essay by the editor and extensive bibliographical material. A most important reference.

15. Weber, Adna F. *The Growth of Cities in the Nineteenth Century.* See No. 86.

B. ECOLOGICAL VARIABLES AND THEIR INTERRELATIONSHIPS

Collected Works

16. Barnett, Lincoln and the editors of Life. *The World We Live In.* Vol. 3. *The Earth and the Universe.* New York: Time, Inc., 1962. 319 pp. **S**

This book contains several articles on natural regions such as the rain forest, arctic barrens, and the desert. Originally published as a series in *Life Magazine*. Useful for studying the nature of eco-systems and acquainting students with various aspects of the environment. Excellent photographs.

17. Chorley, Richard J. and Peter Haggett. *Frontiers in Geographical Teaching*. London: Methuen and Co., Ltd., 1965. 378 pp.

Well written exploration of new developments in geography and their teaching problems. Chapter 4, "Geography and Population," emphasizes the reciprocal relationship between population distribution and economic activity, and includes a useful case study. Chapter 5, "Trends in Social Geography," considers "spatial manifestations of social change," particularly in urban and metropolitan regions. Very little methodology for secondary schools, but nevertheless extremely worthwhile.

18. Davis, Kingsley, ed. *A Crowding Hemisphere: Population Change in the Americas*. Vol. 316. *Annals of the Academy of Political and Social Science*. March 1958. 197 pp.

A collection of statistically oriented readings dealing with recent population trends in Canada, the United States, and Latin America. Determinants of population change are considered. Articles dealing with urbanization are most relevant. General trends only. Teachers.

19. Freedman, Ronald. *Population: The Vital Revolution*. New York: Doubleday, 1964. 274 pp. **Pa S**

A collection of nineteen essays, concerned mainly with demographic processes and population trends for specific regions and for the world as a whole. Narrow in scope, but clear and non-technical. Several articles are appropriate for high school use, especially Chapter 5, "World Urbanization," Chapter 6, "Taking an Inventory of 180 Million People: The U. S. Census," and Chapter 9, "Internal Migration and Population Redistribution in the United States."

20. *Hauser, Philip M. and Otis Dudley Duncan. *The Study of Population: An Inventory and Appraisal*. Chicago: University of Chicago Press, 1959. 864 pp.

Twenty-eight scholars representing several disciplines investigate the nature, methods, past development, and future of demography, in order to evaluate its mid–twentieth-century status. Part 4, particularly valuable for our purposes, includes articles examining the relationship between demography and other disciplines; the most noteworthy are cited here. A monumental work, with particularly excellent selected bibliographies.

21. Scientific American. *Technology and Economic Development*. New York: Alfred A. Knopf, 1963. 194 pp.

The role of technology in the development of "non-industrial" countries receives primary emphasis in this unique book of readings. Several articles pursue the interrelationship of technology and other ecological variables as they relate to economic development. See especially: "Food" by Nevin S. Scrimshaw, "Water" by Roger Revelle, and "Population" by Kingsley Davis.

22. Spengler, Joseph J. and Otis D. Duncan. *Demographic Analysis: Selected Readings*. Glencoe, Illinois: The Free Press, 1956. 783 pp.

An anthology of short scholarly readings on all aspects of population study, most of which take the "narrow" demographic point of view. Chapters 5 and 6 relate population to other variables and are more broad in scope; see especially "The Process of Urbanization" by Hope T. Eldridge.

23. Thomas, William L., ed. *Man's Role in Changing the Face of the Earth*. Chicago: University of Chicago Press, 1956. 1193 pp.

A massive compilation of articles; the product of an interdisciplinary symposium emphasizing how man's technology and organization have influenced the environment. Includes case studies for several world regions. Teachers.

General and Special Works

24. Ackerman, Edward A. "Population and Natural Resources." Philip M. Hauser and Otis Dudley Duncan, eds. *The Study of Population; An Inventory and Appraisal*. Chicago: University of Chicago Press, 1959, pp. 621–647.

Considers technology and culture as mediating factors in the population-resource relationship. Discusses the reciprocal relationship between density, distribution and resource development. Excellent examples are provided. Important statement, but somewhat technical.

25. Alexander, John W. *Economic Geography*. Englewood Cliffs, New Jersey: Prentice-Hall, 1963. 647 pp.

A reputable general text, including a short analysis of world population distribution in Chapter 2, "People, the Producers and Consumers." Raises interesting questions concerning the changing interrelationship of man, his technology, culture, and resources.

26. Anderson, R. C. "The Role of Human Geography in the Study of Emerging Nations." *Social Education,* 29:331–337, October 1965.

How the study of population can aid students in understanding the growth of underdeveloped nations. Methods are suggested. See especially "Man-Land Relationships in Underdeveloped Nations," which stresses how technology, culture, and social organization mediate between the population and its environment. Excellent for HS. and JHS. teachers.

27. Beshers, James M. *Population Processes and Social Systems.* New York: Free Press, 1967.

An advanced and detailed treatment of demography from the standpoint that social controls, as contrasted with Malthusian types of environmental controls, are of the utmost importance in understanding population phenomena.

28. Bogue, Donald J. "Population Distribution." Philip M. Hauser and Otis Dudley Duncan, eds. *The Study of Population: An Inventory and Appraisal.* Chicago: University of Chicago Press, 1959, pp. 383–399.

A review of population distribution research and methodology, with an outline of principles for delimiting areal units. Advocates local regional study and stresses importance of co-variant analysis. Important sections consider how variations in physical environment, social conditions, and economic organization exert influence on population distribution. Excellent introduction to this field. Extensive bibliography.

29. *Broek, Jan O. M. *Geography: Its Scope and Spirit* (Social Science Seminar Series). Columbus, Ohio: Charles E. Merrill Books, 1965. 116 pp. **Pa**

A simple, clear introduction to all aspects of geography. Concise outline of the "Geographic Aspects of Population," pp. 34–42, including distribution, growth, density, and movement. Includes up-to-date quantitative techniques and mapping methods, pp. 60–71, many of which may be used in teaching population in secondary school. Valuable for teachers.

30. Brunhes, Jean. *Human Geography.* Chicago: Rand McNally, 1920. 648 pp.

An old but classic study of man's relationship to his environment, notable for its analyses of small "natural units," several of which are appropriate as bases for regional case studies. Includes material on the desert communities of the M'zab and Suf of the Sahara, the highland communities of the central Andes, and the Balearic Island communities of Majorca and Minorca.

31. Clark, Colin. "Transportation—Maker and Breaker of Cities." *Town Planning Review*, 28: 237–250, January 1958.

Somewhat less exciting than the title would lead one to believe. Historical survey of the role of transportation in city development, industrial location and population distribution. Some troublesome economic terminology. Teachers.

32. Clarke, John I. *Population Geography*. London: Pergamon Press, 1965. 164 pp. **Pa**

A narrow view of the discipline of population geography, considering environmental conditions as major determinants of population distribution. Most useful to the teacher unfamiliar with population dynamics, demographic definitions, and measures of distribution and density. Large portion devoted to the "demographic processes."

33. Cook, Robert C. "Pitfalls of Progress." *The Nation*, 194: 31–33, January 13, 1962. **S**

A comment by a demographer, indicating that present technology is not producing enough resources for human needs. Narrow demographic view, overly restricted in scope. Interesting material for student analysis and criticism, using the tools of ecology.

34. Firey, Walter. *Land Use in Central Boston* (Harvard Sociological Studies, Vol. 4). Cambridge: Harvard University Press, 1947. 367 pp.

A fascinating theoretical and empirical study of values and sentiments as they affect land use patterns and population distributions. Actually, a consideration of the social psychological factor in the ecosystem. For teachers.

35. Firey, Walter. "Sentiment and Symbolism as Ecological Variables." *American Sociological Review*, 10: 140–148, April 1945. **B-M Reprint S-85**

One of the first articles to consider cultural values as determinants of land use patterns and spatial distributions. A consideration of the social psychological dimension of the ecological complex. Teachers only.

36. Gibbs, Jack P. "The Evolution of Population Concentration." *Economic Geography*, 39: 119–129, April 1963.

A five-step theory of population concentration, with reference to technological and economic factors which occur at each step (pp. 119–122). Remainder of the article presents a test of the model. For teachers.

37. Gilmore, Harlan. *Transportation and the Growth of Cities.* Glencoe, Illinois: The Free Press, 1953. 146 pp. S

How changes in transportation affected the location, size, and functions of cities from ancient times to the present. Major emphasis on changes in function and distribution of activities within the city, with only some description of population mix and distribution. Economic orientation. Portions suitable for HS use.

38. Ginsburg, Norton. "Natural Resources and Economic Development." *Association of American Geographers, Annals*, 47: 196–212, September 1957.

See "Natural Resources: The Fifth Element in Economic Development," for an explanation of the role played by social organization and technology in determining what constitutes a resource. An all-important concept. For teachers.

39. Halbwachs, Maurice. *Population and Society.* Tr. Otis Dudley Duncan and Harold W. Pfautz. Glencoe, Illinois: The Free Press, 1960.

A sophisticated if somewhat difficult study by a French sociologist, noting the reciprocal relationship between population phenomena and social factors. Recognizes "collective psychology" as an influential force. A perceptive work.

40. Hawley, Amos H. "Population Composition." Philip M. Hauser and Otis Dudley Duncan, eds. *The Study of Population: An Inventory and Appraisal.* Chicago: University of Chicago Press, 1959, pp. 361–382.

A description of common population characteristics and methods of compilation and analysis. How population characteristics are indicators of local economy and culture. Technical demographic terminology unimportant for present use. See especially Part 1. Teachers.

41. Hertzberg, Hazel W. *Teaching Population Dynamics* (Population Instructional Materials Project, International Studies Program). New York: Teachers College, Columbia University, 1965. 91 pp. **Pa**

One of the few publications attempting to bring demographic methodology and understanding into the classroom. Concerned with population in its "narrow" sense, but provides material on problems, definitions, and tools of population study necessary for teaching population in any context.

42. *Hunker, Henry L. *Erich W. Zimmermann's Introduction to World Resources.* New York: Harper and Row, 1964. 211 pp. **Pa**

An invaluable work, concentrating on the dynamic relationship between resources and the social organization and technology of a society. See Chapter 1, "The Meaning and Nature of Resources," for a concise summary of the thesis. Population distribution is the theme of Chapter 8, "Man and Resources," and of particular importance is the passage "Man-Land Ratio and Population Density" (pp. 137–140). This publication of the first ten chapters of Zimmermann's original work is a clear, comprehensible exposition of the interrelationship of resources, culture, and man.

43. James, Preston E. "The Geographical Study of Population." Preston E. James and Clarence F. Jones, eds. *American Geography; Inventory and Prospect.* Syracuse: Syracuse University Press, 1954, pp. 106–122.

A discussion of the scope, objectives, problems, and completed and suggested research in the field of population geography in 1954. Rather outdated, but comments on population mapping and analysis are still relevant.

44. Leontief, Wassily W. "Input-Output Economics." *Scientific American,* 185: 15–21, October 1951. **SA–610**

One of the earlier articles exploring input-output analysis. A brief but clear introduction. Should be supplemented by more recent publications (see Nos. 45 and 46). Teachers.

45. Leontief, Wassily W. "The Structure of Development." Scientific American, *Technology and Economic Development.* New York: Alfred A. Knopf, 1963, pp. 105–124. **SA–617**

A brief but technical explanation of the methods and functions of input-output analysis. Stress is on economic structure as an indicator of technological level of development. See also the author's recent *Input-Output Economics* (New York: Oxford University Press, 1966, 257 pp.).

46. Leontief, Wassily. "The Structure of the American Economy." *Scientific American,* 212: 25–35, April 1965. **SA–624**

A clear explanation of input-output analysis, using the American economy as a case in point. Illustrates how to interpret input-output tables.

47. Lynch, Kevin. *The Image of the City.* Cambridge, Mass: MIT Press, 1960. 194 pp. **Pa**

A pioneer work describing how urbanites perceive the physical forms of the city and how certain elements in the cityscape contribute to its "legibility." A solid contribution to the understanding of the role of social psychology in urban life.

48. Ogburn, William F. "Technology as Environment." In Otis Dudley Duncan, ed. *William F. Ogburn, On Culture and Social Change.* Chicago: University of Chicago Press, 1964, pp. 78–85. **S B-M Reprint S–212**

A clearly written essay emphasizing the influence of technology upon man's social life, including migration, population growth, and stability of residence. Stresses direct and indirect adaptations to a technological environment. Readable for HS students.

49. Ogburn, William F. "Inventions, Population and History." In Otis Dudley Duncan, ed. *William F. Ogburn on Culture and Social Change.* Chicago: University of Chicago Press, 1964, pp. 62–77. **S B-M Reprint S–474**

How inventions, both mechanical and social, affect population size, land use, city growth, migration, division of labor, and social stratification. Narrow scope, with emphasis on technology as a social force to the exclusion of other variables. Several passages are extremely useful. HS reading level.

50. *Olmstead, Clarence W. "People, Time, Space and Ideas: I." *Social Education,* 22: 15–19, January 1958.

Stresses the importance of "ideas" (technology and culture) as factors influencing the distribution of man in "space." Also includes a clear explanation of the dynamic concept of resources. Well written, informative, and important. For teachers.

51. Pounds, Norman J. G. *The Earth and You.* Chicago: Rand-McNally, 1962. 591 pp. **S**

An impressive work, written for youngsters by a distinguished geographer, with a worthwhile chapter summarizing the reasons for the unequal distribution of the world's population. Appropriate for JHS use.

52. Spoehr, Alexander. "Cultural Differences in the Interpretation of Natural Resources." In William L. Thomas, ed., *Man's Role in Changing the Face of the Earth.* Chicago: University of Chicago Press, 1956, pp. 93–102.

A discussion of the role of technology, social structure, and habitat in determining man's relationship to resources. Should be read in conjunction with Zimmermann's *World Resources and Industries.* Cross-cultural examples cited.

53. United Nations, Department of Social Affairs, Population Division. *The Determinants and Consequences of Population Trends* (Population Studies, No. 17). New York: Columbia University Press, 1954. 404 pp.

A vast collection of findings on the relationship between economic and social factors and population trends. "Narrow" scope, with only superficial consideration of geographical and technological factors.

54. Wrong, Dennis H. *Population and Society.* New York: Random House, 1961. 115 pp. **Pa**

A short work, narrow in scope and devoted primarily to historical and world-wide trends in the "demographic processes" of fertility, mortality, and migration. Useful overview of these aspects of population study.

55. *Zelinsky, Wilbur. *A Prologue to Population Geography.* Englewood Cliffs, New Jersey: Prentice-Hall, Inc., 1966. 150 pp. **Pa**

A tentative but perceptive exploration of the nature, scope, structure, and methods of population geography. Takes a significantly broad view of the determinants of population size and distribution by considering the following factors: physical environment, economy, cultural configuration, physical and social disasters, and impact of specific social and political decisions. The best of the few monographs devoted to this relatively new field.

C. THE ECOLOGICAL APPROACH TO
URBAN REGIONS

Collected Works

56. Davis, Kingsley, ed. *A Crowding Hemisphere: Population Change in the Americas.* See No. 18.

57. Getis, Arthur and Judith Getis, eds. Urban Geography Issue. *The Journal of Geography,* 45, May 1966.

Written expressly for the secondary school teacher, this remarkable issue summarizes in a clear and non-technical manner several important urban geographical concepts. Topics covered include: present trends in urban geography, the origin and growth of cities, Christaller's Theory of Central Places, and functions and problems of the Central Business District. A well executed effort to bring technical material into the classroom. A must for teachers concerned with urban populations. Reprints of the issue are available from The National Council for Geographic Education, Illinois State University, Normal, Illinois, 61761. (Topics in Geography Series, No. 1)

58. Gist, Noel P. and Sylvia Fleis Fava. *Urban Society.* See No. 4.

59. Glaab, Charles N. *The American City; A Documentary History.* Homewood, Illinois: The Dorsey Press, 1963. 478 pp. S

Several of the essays in this collection contain material on urban population growth and distribution, especially for the 19th century. See, for example, "Transport and the Growth of Cities, 1800–1850" (pp. 70–71), "Adna F. Weber on Urbanization, 1899" (pp. 180–187), "Suburbs (Chicago, 1873)" (pp. 229–232), and "Graham Taylor on Industrial Suburbs, 1915" (pp. 431–439). Particularly recommended because of suitability for HS and advanced JHS students.

60. *Hatt, Paul K. and Albert J. Reiss, eds. *Cities and Society.* Glencoe, Illinois: Free Press, 1961. 852 pp.

An outstanding reader in urban sociology, with an interdisciplinary approach and an emphasis on urban ecology, demography, and social organization. Includes recent and significant papers on urban life by some of America's most eminent sociologists, geographers, and historians. The following sections are most relevant: "The Nature of the City"; "The Nature and Extent of Urbanization and Population Redistribution"; "The History of Urban Settlement"; "The Spatial and Temporal Patterns of Cities"; "Institutional and Organizational Structures and Processes"; "The City as an Artifact."

51

61. Hauser, Philip M., ed. World urbanism issue, *American Journal of Sociology,* 60, March 1955.

A special issue of the Journal devoted to recent studies concerning urban populations and institutions, including the growth of world urbanization, the nature of the preindustrial city, and the nature of American urbanism. Particularly relevant articles are noted.

62. Mayer, Harold M. and Clyde E. Kohn, eds. *Readings in Urban Geography.* Chicago: University of Chicago Press, 1959. 625 pp.

This collection of articles and papers by geographers and specialists in other disciplines is an effort to familiarize readers with the basic concepts of city growth, structure, distribution, and functions. A basic source for teachers seeking a background in the geography of the city.

63. *U. S. Department of Commerce, *The Automobile and Air Pollution, a Program for Progress.* Superintendent of Documents, Washington, D. C.

A searching interdisciplinary study of the effects of air pollution from automobiles on metropolitan regions. Filled with useful visual material for the opaque projector. Volume 1, $.60, Volume 2, $1.00, October 1967 and December 1967 respectively.

General and Specialized Works

64. Adams, Robert M. "The Origin of Cities." *Scientific American,* 203: 153–168, September 1960. **S SA–606**

The thesis of this eminent archeologist is that ancient cities grew in response to new patterns in social organization. Estimates the development of social stratification and population size, mix, and distribution in the cities of Mesopotamia, and enumerates the economic, social, and technological conditions which fostered these developments. Advanced.

65. Allen, Frederick Lewis. "The Big Change in Suburbia." *Harper's Magazine,* 208: 21–28, June 1954. **S**

Popular account of "urban decentralization" in the United States. Considers five stages of suburban growth, from the era of settlement along railroad and trolley lines to the era of suburbanization of business. Unanalytical, but readable for JHS and SHS students. Considers the role of values and technology in suburban growth.

66. Bogue, Donald J. "The Structure of the Metropolitan Community."

George Theodorson, ed. *Studies in Human Ecology.* Evanston, Illinois: Row Peterson and Company, 1961, pp. 524–538.

A discussion of how the interrelationship of several variables affects the patterning of activities and population in the metropolis.

67. Bogue, Donald J. *The Structure of the Metropolitan Community.* Ann Arbor: University of Michigan, 1949. 210 pp.

A well known, but tediously detailed, effort to test the hypothesis of metropolitan dominance, using the U. S. in 1940 as a basis for study. Human ecological approach, but somewhat complex for present purposes. Teachers only.

68. Davis, Kingsley. "The Origin and Growth of Urbanization in the World." *American Journal of Sociology,* 60: 429–437, March 1955. **B-M Reprint S–66**

A celebrated study of urban trends from ancient times to 1950. Discussion of the technological innovations and changes in social organization which contributed to the rise of Neolithic cities. Review of recent trends in world urbanization from 1800–1950, including types and rates of growth and processes of "metropolitanization."

69. *Dickinson, Robert E. *City and Region: A Geographical Interpretation.* London: Routledge and Kegan Paul, Ltd., 1964. 576 pp.

A comprehensive survey of urban and metropolitan regions by a distinguished geographer, emphasizing spatial distributions and ecological structure. Probably the best study of its kind. Considers the growth, structure, and interrelationships of the areas of the "city-region." Case studies from the United States and Western Europe, suitable for classroom use, support much of the material. Rich collection of population distribution maps and diagrams. Highly recommended for teachers.

70. Foley, Donald L. "Urban Daytime Population: A Field for Demographic and Ecological Analysis." *Social Forces,* 32: 323–330, May 1954.

How technological, historical, and economic factors affect the spatial distribution of urban daytime populations. Review and discussion of research on recurrent urban population movements. For teachers.

71. Friedmann, John. "Cities in Social Transformation." John Friedmann and William Alonso, eds. *Regional Development and Planning.* Cambridge: MIT Press, 1964, pp. 343–360.

A sophisticated article dealing with several new concepts in urban studies, including the city as a cross-cultural type and the functional hierarchy of cities. Relevant to understanding the distribution of population and economic activities in urban areas. See "The Growth of Cities," pp. 350–351, for an excellent summary of the effect of technological innovations on population growth. More simplified material should be read first, but a stab at this article is well worth it. Teachers.

72. Gist, Noel P. "Developing Patterns of Urban Decentralization." *Social Forces,* 30: 257–267, March 1952.

How technological, economic, and social psychological factors operate in the trend toward decentralization of urban populations; based on a case study of a group of urban-occupied families living in open country outside Columbia, Missouri. Social psychological factors are stressed.

73. Gras, N. S. B. "The Development of the Metropolitan Economy in Europe and America." George Theodorson, ed. *Studies in Human Ecology.* Evanston, Illinois: Row Peterson and Company, 1961, pp. 516–524.

A classic statement on metropolitan growth and dominance.

74. Haagen-Smit, A. J. "The Control of Air Pollution." *Scientific American,* 208, January 1964. **SA–618**

Already somewhat dated—the problem is deepening so fast—but recommended because of its easy availability.

75. Hoyt, Homer. "The Residential and Retail Patterns of Leading Latin American Cities." *Land Economics,* 39: 449–454, November 1963.

An outline of the distribution of residential populations and economic activities in selected Latin American cities. Brings the account of changes in urban spatial patterns up to date, and considers how topography, technology, and the city itself influence distribution. A short, factual summary.

76. Lynch, Kevin. "The Form of Cities." *Scientific American,* 190: 54–63, April 1954. **S**

What a city's size, density, structural pattern, and physical shape tell us about the character of the city and its population. How people shape these properties, and how in turn they are shaped by them. Comparisons of ancient and modern, western and non-western cities. Excellent aerial photographs complement the text. Advanced HS. Unique approach.

77. Lynch, Kevin. *The Image of the City.* See No. 47.

78. McDermott, Walsh. "Air Pollution and Public Health." *Scientific American,* 205, October 1961. **SA–612**

An exploration of an important area of destructive environmental transformation on the part of technological man.

79. McKenzie, Roderick D. *The Metropolitan Community.* New York: McGraw Hill, 1933. 352 pp.

An old but classic work, developing the concept of the metropolitan community, with many geographical and ecological insights. Considers technological and cultural factors as primary determinants of urban growth, expansion, and population distribution, emphasizing the role of transportation innovation. Descriptive and statistical materials are outdated, but the basic concepts of "metropolitanization" are classic. Teachers.

80. Park, R. E., E. W. Burgess and R. D. McKenzie. *The City.* See No. 9.

81. Park, R. E. *Human Communities.* See No. 10.

82. Reissman, Leonard. "The Ecologists—Analysts of Urban Patterns." See No. 11.

83. *Scientific American. Cities.* New York: Alfred A. Knopf, 1965. 211 pp. **Pa**

This reprint of the September 1965 issue of *Scientific American* contains readings on urban transportation, land use, growth, and planning. Several articles are applicable to the ecological study of urban populations. See especially: "The Urbanization of Population" by Kingsley Davis; "The Origin and Evolution of Cities" by Gideon Sjoberg; and "The Modern Metropolis" by Hans Blumenfeld. Several other articles provide useful materials for urban case studies. Note that the paperback reprint does not include many of the excellent pictures and aerial photographs contained in the original issue.

84. Sjoberg, Gideon, "The Preindustrial City." *American Journal of Sociology,* 60: 438–445, March 1955. **B-M Reprint S–271**

A summary of some of the major points discussed in the book of the same name. Compares the growth patterns of industrial and pre-industrial cities and describes the spatial structure of the latter. Teachers.

85. *Sjoberg, Gideon. *The Preindustrial City*. Glencoe, Illinois: The Free Press, 1960. 343 pp. **S Pa**

A thorough analysis of a much neglected area, with an ecological orientation. Considers how technology, culture and values, social power, and environment influence the spatial, economic, and social structures of preindustrial cities. An impressive work, with portions appropriate for HS students. A rich source, highly recommended.

86. *Weber, Adna F. *The Growth of Cities in the Nineteenth Century*. Ithaca, New York: Cornell University Press, 1963. 475 pp. **Pa**

A classic study of the processes of urban growth, citing economic variables as primary causal factors of population agglomeration in cities, but recognizing the role of political, social, psychological, and technological variables as well. A work based on solid statistical evidence and demonstrating a perceptive understanding of interrelationships. A forerunner of modern ecological thought. For teachers.

GENERAL AIDS

In order to accumulate data and material for developing regional case studies for classroom use, many sources must be tapped. Where does one acquire information about the population and its characteristics, the level of agricultural technology, the land forms and soils, or the culture of a particular region? This section should be helpful in finding answers to this type of question. Out of the voluminous literature on world regions, we have listed, in Part A, references intended to lead the teacher or student to sources for specific regions, and have cited sample regional studies to indicate the type of material available.

The journals listed in Part B are primarily American publications. Bibliographic listings of serials similar in content, published elsewhere, may be found in Part D. The statistical sources cited in Part C focus on the United States. For other individual countries and states who publish their own statistics, the reader is referred again to bibliographic sources in Part D. Many are not as complete as the American data; the United Nations publications, however, maintain an especially high standard of scholarship. Part D also includes some sample regional bibliographies.

Visual materials for studying population in an ecological context are in extensive supply. Representative materials are cited in Part E. The population distribution maps listed represent but a few of the thousands of local, regional, and national maps to be found in journals, books, articles, and atlases, or to be obtained from city, state, or national agencies. Similarly, only the major population atlases are cited, along with several regional and general atlases. A number of the films and filmstrips noted in Part E are for use with the regional case studies that comprise the final major section of this chapter. Others, depicting plant and animal ecosystems, are useful as background to the study of human ecosystems. When an annotation is not the authors', a parenthetical note following the film or filmstrip citation indicates the name of the guide or bibliography in which the annotation originally appeared.

With these aids the teacher will be able to accumulate material for regional studies, although data on all factors may not be available for every region. Other sources of information include current popular periodicals and newspapers, although they are not listed here, and the bibliographies and general guides to visual materials that conclude Part E.

A. SERIES

87. American Geographical Society. *Around the World Program.* Published irregularly. Garden City, New York: Nelson Doubleday. S

A series of short paperback volumes devoted to various world nations. Provides general information on all aspects of society, along with some excellent pictures. Written specifically for students.

88. Barnett, Lincoln. *The World We Live In.* See No. 16.

89. Fitzsimmons, Thomas, gen. ed. *Survey of World Cultures. Human Relations Area Files.* 13 vols. to date. New Haven: HRAF Press. S

A series of thirteen volumes, each dealing with a world nation, written by interdisciplinary teams. Wealth of material on population, environment, technology, and social organization, but little examination of interrelationships. Written for the student. Advanced JHS and SHS. Countries covered include: Poland, Jordan, Iraq, Saudi Arabia, Cambodia, China, U.S.S.R., Laos, Ethiopia, Cuba, Afghanistan, Indonesia, and Pakistan.

90. *Portrait of the Nations Series.* Philadelphia: J. B. Lippincott. 57 vols. to date. S

A highly readable series, with individual volumes surveying various nations of the world. Contains information on all aspects of society. Especially for students.

B. SERIALS

91. *American Anthropologist.* (1888–). 6 times annually. American Anthropological Association, 1530 P Street, N. W., Washington, D. C. 20005.

Important articles by professional anthropologists, several dealing with the cultural or social ecology of particular regions. Anthropological interpretation of ecology with an emphasis on the role of cultural factors.

92. *American Sociological Review.* (1936–). Bi-monthly. American Sociological Association, 1755 Massachusetts Avenue, N. W., Washington, D. C. 20036.

A scholarly journal devoted to all aspects of sociology. Most articles dealing with population and ecology are narrow in scope and technical in orientation, with much space devoted to methodology. Includes articles devoted to American cities and metropolitan regions.

93. *Association of American Geographers, Annals.* (1913–). **Quarterly.** Association of American Geographers, 1146 Sixteenth Street, N. W., Washington, D. C. 20036.

Scholarly articles on a variety of geographical topics ranging over a multitude of regions. Increasing emphasis on theoretical, methodological, and descriptive items in population geography. Includes many regional articles appropriate as bases for case studies.

94. *Economic Development and Cultural Change.* (1952–). **Quarterly.** (Research Center for Economic Development and Cultural Change). University of Chicago Press, 5750 Ellis Avenue, Chicago, Illinois 60637.

A series of studies, rather technical and narrow in scope, by eminent economists, anthropologists, sociologists, and geographers. Many articles contain useful case study material.

95. *Economic Geography.* (1925–). Quarterly. The Editor, Clark University, 950 Main Street, Worcester, Massachusetts 01610.

The more recent issues tend to include an increasing number of articles on population geography, including the growth and distribution of urban populations in relation to economic activities. Articles range from theoretical to descriptive with many regional studies. Fine source for maps.

96. *Focus.* (1950–). 10 times annually. American Geographical Society, Broadway at 156th Street, New York 10032. **S**

A series of simply written six-page pamphlets, profiling a nation or region or topic of general geographic interest. Each issue includes a set of useful but small scale maps, ranging in subject from transport lines to population distribution. One of the few authoritative, professional serials written for the general reader. For JHS and SHS. Single copies are available from the American Geographical Society.

97. *Geographical Journal* (Royal Geographical Society). (1893–). Quarterly. John Murray Ltd., 50 Albemarle Street, London, W. L. England.

Emphasis on exploration and physical geography, with some attention to population geography. Concentrates on British areas. Case study materials.

98. *Geographical Review* (American Geographical Society of New York). (1916–). Quarterly. American Geographical Society, Broadway at 156th Street, New York, New York 10032.

A scholarly journal, covering all fields of geographic interest, with a growing emphasis on the growth and distribution of population. Includes both theoretical and descriptive articles for various world regions. Excellent source of population maps. Provides both yearly and cumulative indexes.

99. *Journal of Tropical Geography* (Published by the Departments of Geography, University of Singapore and University of Malaya). (1953–). 2 times annually. Department of Geography, University of Singapore, Cluny Road, Singapore 10, Malaysia.

Includes excellent articles on Southeast Asia and Africa, many useful for case study material. Example of the type of journal to check when seeking regional data.

100. *Population Bulletin.* (1944–). 8 times annually. Population Reference Bureau, 1755 Massachusetts Avenue, N. W., Washington, D. C. 20036.

A demographic journal, with a "population problems" orientation, rather narrow in scope. Provides some useful source data concerning composition and distribution in a variety of world regions.

101. *Population Index.* (1935–). Quarterly. Office of Population Research, Woodrow Wilson School of Public and International Affairs, Princeton, New Jersey (for the Population Association of America).

Includes articles, charts, statistics, and an annotated bibliography listing primarily demographic articles, with some interdisciplinary material. Good source for listings of official statistical publications.

102. *Scientific American.* (1845–). Monthly. Scientific American, Inc., 415 Madison Avenue, New York, New York 10017.

This highly reputable science journal contains frequent articles in the social sciences. Many selections on population, urbanization, anthropology, and economics are relevant to the study of ecology. Several of these are cited in the bibliography, some of which are available as inexpensive reprints ($.20 apiece) from W. H. Freeman and Company, 660 Market Street, San Francisco, California. If a reading is available as a reprint, that fact is noted in the annotation. Many reprints do not include the pictures and aerial photographs included in the original article.

103. *Scottish Geographical Magazine* (Royal Scottish Geographical Society). (1885–). 3 numbers annually. The Royal Scottish Geographical Society, 10 Randolph Crescent, Edinburgh 3, Scotland.

For articles on population geography and the relationship of population to other variables for specific regions, the teacher should check publications of the area in question. This scholarly journal concentrates on the British Isles and Commonwealth countries, in particular, Scotland. Includes many articles appropriate for case studies.

104. *Social Forces.* (1922–). Quarterly. University of North Carolina Press, Chapel Hill, North Carolina 27515.

A scholarly sociology journal, broader in scope and less technical in orientation than other journals of its kind. Includes frequent articles on human ecology and urban growth and development.

C. STATISTICAL SOURCES

105. Adams, Thomas, Harold M. Lewis and Theodore T. McKrosky.
     Population, Land Values and Government. Vol. 2. *Regional Plan
     of New York and Its Environs, 1929.* New York: Regional Plan
     of New York, 1929. 320 pp.

     Contains a historical, descriptive account of population trends in
     the greater New York region for the period. Considers factors that
     influence grow:h and distribution, such as transport, land values,
     and commerce. Maps of transit lines, land values, and distributions
     and densities are mediocre, but useful. Good reference material for
     teachers concerned with New York City.

106. Bogue, Donald J. *The Population of the United States.* New
     York: Free Press of Glencoe, 1959. 859 pp.

     An encyclopedic reference work, written for the general reader, with
     an emphasis on changes from 1950–1960. Consult especially Part
     I, which deals with population distribution. Charts and tables,
     dispersed throughout the text, are useful for student analysis.

107. Hauser, Philip M. "The Census of 1960." *Scientific American,*
     205: 39–45, July 1961. **S**

     A very general summary of significant population changes in the
     United States, inferred from the 1960 census. Includes trends in
     redistribution, composition, and growth. Demographic orientation,
     but an excellent source of charts and graphs depicting change.

108. New York Herald Tribune. *The U. S. Book of Facts, Statistics
     and Information.* New York: Pocket Books, Inc., 1965. 106 pp.
     Pa

     Contains the complete and unabridged *Statistical Abstract of the
     United States, 1965,* including a guide to the principal sources of
     statistical information for individual states. Handy, inexpensive
     ($1.95) reference book for teachers.

109. New York State Department of Commerce. Research Bulletin
     No. 7. *Basic Statistics for Counties and Metropolitan Areas of
     New York State, 1964.* Albany: New York State Department of
     Commerce, 1964.

     Short statistical summaries of general population characteristics
     and business, manufacturing, and agricultural data for each county
     and metropolitan area in New York State. Includes changes in

population size and manufacturing employment and a graph of population change from 1860–1960. An extremely useful state publication. Free from the State Department of Commerce or regional and branch offices.

110. New York State Department of Commerce. *State and Area Fact Book*. Albany: State Department of Commerce, 1963. **S**

A summary of population, housing, business, and manufacturing statistics for major economic areas, including data for counties, communities, and SMSA's* within each area. Simple written introductory text with charts and graphs is suitable for JHS and HS students. Useful compilation for study of local communities. Example of helpful publications distributed by state governments. For free copy write: New York State Department of Commerce, 112 State Street, Albany, New York 12207, or a regional or branch office.

111. Steinberg, S. H. *The Statesman's Yearbook, 1968–1969*. New York: St. Martin's Press, 1968. 1732 pp.

This annual provides a handy statistical and historical summary for each state of the world. To each national summary is appended a list of important reference works, including statistical sources. In most cases, the address of the national office of statistics is also appended.

112. United Nations Statistical Office. *Demographic Yearbook*. New York: United Nations. Annual since 1948.

A highly accessible source of international population statistics. Each volume in the series emphasizes a particular aspect of demography, including data concerning the composition, distribution and growth of over 250 geographical areas of the world. Usefulness limited by lack of data for small regions or civil divisions. Cumulative index included in Volume 16, 1964.

113. U. S. Department of Commerce, Bureau of the Census. *County and City Data Book, 1967*. Washington: U. S. Government Printing Office, 1967.

An abstract of social and economic statistics for civil divisions and small regions in the United States, including states, counties, Standard Metropolitan Statistical Areas, urbanized areas, and cities. Available in most libraries.

* SMSA is the abbreviation for Standard Metropolitan Statistical Area.

114. U. S. Department of Commerce, Bureau of the Census. *Historical Statistics of the United States: Colonial Times to 1957.* Washington, D. C.: U. S. Government Printing Office, 1960. 774 pp.

A general reference work, with statistics outlining the economic and social development of the nation, compiled from various sources. See especially chapters on population, labor force, minerals, transportation, communication, and wholesale and retail trade. Clothbound issues may be purchased at $6.00 a copy from Superintendent of Documents, U. S. Government Printing Office, Washington, D. C.

115. U. S. Department of Commerce, Bureau of the Census. *Statistical Abstract of the United States.* 86 vols. 1878–1966. Washington: U. S. Government Printing Office.

An annual summary of social, political, and economic statistics, compiled from various census and non-census sources. Primarily national data, but provides addresses where state materials may be obtained; see Guide to State Statistical Abstracts.

116. U. S. Department of Commerce, Bureau of the Census. *U. S. Census of Housing, 1960.* Vol. 3. *City Blocks.* Series HC(3). Washington: U. S. Government Printing Office, 1961.

Detailed statistics on characteristics of housing units, by city blocks, published for those cities with 50,000 or more inhabitants.

117. U. S. Department of Commerce, Bureau of the Census. *U. S. Census of Population, 1960. Subject Reports.* Series PC(2). Washington: U. S. Government Printing Office, 1963.

A compilation of detailed statistics, arranged by subject, and organized according to regional, local, and urban and rural divisions. Particularly noteworthy are:

Non-White Population by Race	PC(2)-1C
Occupation by Industry	PC(2)-7C
Occupational Characteristics	PC(2)-7A
Lifetime and Recent Migration	PC(2)-2D

118. U. S. Department of Commerce, Bureau of the Census. *U. S. Census of Population and Housing, 1960. Census Tracts.* Series PHC(1). 180 parts. Washington: U. S. Government Printing Office, 1962.

A source of major importance for United States statistics, organized according to Standard Metropolitan Statistical Areas. Includes data on general characteristics, age, color, marital status, labor force characteristics, characteristics of non-white population, and housing characteristics, for each tract. Reports on individual SMSA's may be purchased at varying costs from Superintendent of Documents, U. S. Government Printing Office, Washington, D. C. 20401.

119. U. S. Department of the Interior, Bureau of Mines. *1963 Minerals Yearbook.* Vol. 4. Area Reports: International. Washington: U. S. Government Printing Office, 1964. 1505 pp.

A useful review of minerals in the world economy, including statistics for more than 130 countries and areas. This is the last edition of the yearbook to include detailed background information on the resources of individual nations. Lists source material for each country.

120. Wattenberg, Ben J. and Richard M. Scammon. *This U. S. A.* Garden City: Doubleday and Company, 1965. 520 pp.

A study of contemporary population trends in the United States, based on census publications and written for the general reader. Concerned with recent trends in population size, distribution, movement, and migration. More descriptive than analytical, but includes useful general statistical data.

121. Woytinsky, Wladimir S. and Emma S. Woytinsky. *World Population and Production: Trends and Outlook.* New York: Twentieth Century Fund, 1953. 1268 pp.

This gargantuan undertaking is limited by a rather unanalytical text, but is useful for its massive compilation of maps, charts and diagrams. It contains a descriptive "outline" of world economic and demographic trends.

D. BIBLIOGRAPHIES

122. American Geographical Society. *Current Geographical Publications.* Ed. Nordis Felland. New York: A. G. S. (1938–). Mimeo. Monthly except July and August.

Additions to the Research Catalog of the American Geographical Society are indexed by subject and region. Teachers should check index for "Geography of Population" or "Human Geography."

123. Berry, Brian J. L. and Allan Pred. *Central Place Studies; a Bibliography of Theory and Applications* (Regional Science Research Institute. Bibliography Series, No. 1). Philadelphia: Re-

gional Science Research Institute, 1965. 153 pp. Also: Barnum, H. G., et. al. *Supplement through 1964.* 50 pp. (1965).

Included as an introduction to this annotated bibliography is a review of the theory of central places as developed by Walter Christaller. Chapter 13 lists ecological publications which are specifically related to central place theory.

124. *Church, Martha, Robert E. Huke and Wilbur Zelinsky. *A Basic Geographical Library: A Selected and Annotated Book List for American Colleges* (A. A. G. Commission on College Geography, Publication No. 2). Washington, D. C.: Association of American Geographers, 1966. 153 pp.

An excellent compilation of general geographical works on all aspects of the discipline, directed toward the undergraduate population. The four principal sections are: General Works and Aids, Geographical Methods, Thematic Geography, and Regional Geography. The latter is an invaluable tool for developing case studies, for it includes bibliographies, serials, atlases, general, special, and regional works for the major world regions. A must for every geography teacher.

125. Eldridge, Hope T. *The Materials of Demography: A Selected and Annotated Bibliography.* New York: Columbia University Press, 1959. 222 pp.

A compilation of the literature through 1958, limited by a narrow demographic scope. Citations of periodicals and serials (Part 1) and of statistical sources and bibliographies (Part 8) will be useful to the teacher.

126. Harris, Chauncy D. *Annotated World List of Selected Current Geographical Serials in English* (University of Chicago, Department of Geography, Research Paper No. 96). Chicago: University of Chicago, 1964. 32 pp.

A selected and annotated bibliography, including serials partly or wholly in English.

127. *Harris, Chauncy D. and Jerome D. Fellman. *International List of Geographical Serials.* (University of Chicago. Department of Geography, Research Paper No. 63). Chicago: University of Chicago, 1960. 194 pp.

A comprehensive listing of geographical serials, both English and non-English, arranged according to country of publication. Should be consulted by teachers seeking information for a particular country or region.

128. *International Bibliography of Sociology.* (1952–   ). Quarterly. UNESCO Publications Center, 317 E. 34th Street, New York, New York, 10016.

A helpful series published by UNESCO, citing sociological material from international sources. See especially sections on "Ecology" and "Social Change," and pp. 187–266, Vol. 1, No. 4, "Social Implications of Technical Advance." Lists national distributors of UNESCO publications.

129. *International Bibliography of Social and Cultural Anthropology.* (1955–   ). Quarterly. UNESCO Publications Center, 317 E. 34th Street, New York, New York, 10016.

One of five sections of an International Bibliography concerned mainly with anthropology, but with relevant geographical and sociological citations. See especially "Ecology" and "Technical Equipment," as well as specific regions. Includes major international publications, many of which are non-English.

130. Long, M., ed. *Handbook for Geography Teachers.* London: Methuen and Company, Ltd., 1964. 533 pp.

Contains an excellent annotated bibliography of all sorts of geographic materials. Comprehensive listing of atlases, visual aids, statistical sources, and journals, many appropriate for population study. Includes where to write for official publications in various countries. Handy guide for teachers seeking case study materials.

131. McManis, Douglas R. *Historical Geography of the United States: A Bibliography.* Ypsilanti, Michigan: Division of Field Services, Eastern Michigan University, 1965. 249 pp.

A comprehensive listing, with a regional-topical organization, focusing on references to material covering the period from historic times to 1900. Useful for collecting materials for U. S. case studies.

132. *Population Research Center, Department of Sociology, University of Texas. *International Population Census Bibliography.* Austin, Texas: Bureau of Business Research, University of Texas.

In order to facilitate location of census materials for research, the Population Research Center is compiling lists of existing census reports, by major world regions. To date, catalogs have been published for Latin America and the Carribean (No. 1), Africa (No. 2), Oceania (No. 3), and North America (No. 4). Each volume is arranged by country. To order, write Bureau of Business Research, University of Texas, Austin, Texas 78712.

133. Quinn, James A. "Topical Summary of Current Literature on Human Ecology." *American Journal of Sociology*, 46: 191–226, September 1940. **B-M Reprint S–481**

A collection of titles by sociologists on various aspects of human ecology, plus a bibliographic essay. The scope of ecology has changed greatly since the time of publication, but the list may prove useful to a teacher searching for case studies. Cites many of the classics in the field.

134. Shannon, Lyle W., ed. "Social Factors in Economic Growth." *Current Sociology*, 6: 173–235, 1957.

Contains an annotated bibliography of recent books and articles, including significant works concerning the relationship of demography to economic growth.

135. UNESCO. *Current List of UNESCO Publications, 1965.* Paris, France: UNESCO, 1965. 66 pp.

This current list, published annually, includes books, periodicals, and series from UNESCO. Notes some valuable sources on various world regions. See especially the following sections: "Official Publications" and "Science and Technology." Lists prices and national distributors. For information write UNESCO Publications Center, 317 East 34th Street, New York, New York 10016.

136. UNESCO. *Sourcebook for Geography Teaching.* See No. 154.

137. **United Nations Publications, 1945–1963.* New York: United Nations, 1964. 71 pp.

A reference catalogue, with sections devoted to demography and international statistics. Lists distributors of U. N. publications throughout the world. Particularly strong on economic data. Supplements available. Write United Nations, Sales Section, Publishing Service, United Nations Plaza, New York, New York 10017.

138. **Zelinsky, Wilbur. *A Bibliographic Guide to Population Geography* (University of Chicago, Department of Geography, Research Paper No. 80). Chicago: University of Chicago, 1962. 257 pp.

A comprehensive bibliography, including citations to general works and a vast listing of regional books and articles, many of which are non-English. Especially useful for teachers seeking information on particular world regions. Includes an introductory essay on the scope and nature of population geography.

139. Zelinsky, Wilbur. "Recent Publications on the Distribution of Population in the United States." *Association of American Geographers, Annals,* 48: 472–481, December 1958.

Review of seventeen publications concerning the spatial distribution of the American population, dealing with metropolitanization and other changes. Excellent summaries and analyses by one of the foremost population geographers.

E. VISUAL AIDS AND TEACHING MATERIALS

Methods

140. Alexander, John W. "An Isarithmic-Dot Population Map." *Economic Geography,* 19: 431–432, October 1943.

Explains the limitations of the dot and isarithmic methods of population mapping, with suggestions for improvement. Useful for students and teachers analyzing or constructing this type of visual.

141. Broek, Jan O. M. *Geography: Its Scope and Spirit.* See No. 29.

142. *Brown, James W., et. al. *A. V. Instruction: Materials and Methods.* 2nd ed. New York: McGraw-Hill Book Company, 1964. 592 pp.

The most comprehensive, up-to-date guide to audio-visual instruction, written expressly to help teachers become acquainted with audio-visual materials. Contains important chapters on creation of materials for classroom use. An excellent reference section describes audio-visual equipment and their operation, and includes a classified directory of sources of visual materials.

143. Hertzberg, Hazel. *Teaching Population Dynamics.* See No. 41.

144. Leuder, Donald R. *Aerial Photographic Interpretation: Principles and Applications.* New York: McGraw-Hill Book Company, 1959. 462 pp.

One of the few general works in the field, including material on principles and practices of aerial photo interpretation as it applies to both terrain and cultural phenomena. Part III demonstrates the use of aerial photography in various fields, including urban and regional studies.

145. *Marsh, Susan. *Teaching About Maps.* 6 vols. Darien, Connecticut: Teachers Publishing Corporation, 1965. **Pa**

An excellent series, written for elementary school teachers, including methods for studying the mapping of population distribution, urban growth, and land use patterns. Population material is scant, but well done. Includes material on interpretation of aerial photographs. Usable at the JHS level. Each chapter includes sources of maps.

146. *Monkhouse, F. J. and H. R. Wilkinson. *Maps and Diagrams: Their Compilation and Construction.* London: Methuen, 1952. 330 pp. 2nd ed., 1963. **Pa**

See Chapter 4, "Population Maps and Diagrams," for a comprehensive survey of techniques for showing population distribution and density. Includes problems and uses of each major type of map. Excellent references, especially for sources of data. Highly recommended for teachers concerned with interpretation of population maps.

147. Murphy, Raymond E. *The American City.* New York: McGraw-Hill Book Company, 1966. 464 pp.

Recent text, especially useful for mapping methods, includes a summary of techniques for studying distribution, density, and social patterns in urban areas (see Chapter 10, "People in the City"). For a useful synopsis of theories of urban growth and expansion, see Chapter 12.

148. Philbrick, Allen K. and Harold M. Mayer. "A Technique for Visual Examination of Association of Areal Patterns." *Journal of Geography*, 50: 367–373, December 1951.

Interesting technique for teaching areal association, using successive slide projections on a base map to record several patterns. This enables the student to view a number of patterns simultaneously and to make inferences as to interrelationships and covariance. Similar techniques can be developed using overhead transparencies with overlays.

149. Robinson, Arthur H. *Elements of Cartography.* 2nd ed. New York: John Wiley and Sons, 1960. 333 pp.

Highly reputable college text in cartography, oriented toward the mapping of areal distributions. Useful aid for those concerned with teaching construction and interpretation of distribution maps. See especially, Chapter 7, pp. 120–124; Chapter 8, pp. 140–147; and Chapter 9.

150. Spurr, Stephen H. *Photogrammetry and Photo Interpretation.* 2nd ed. New York: Ronald Press, 1960. 472 pp.

This textbook, written originally for work in forestry, includes useful sections on the nature and art of aerial photography and the interpretation of aerial photographs. See especially sections on techniques of interpretation for natural phenomena and human activities.

151. Stokes, George A. "The Aerial Photograph: A Key to the Cultural Landscape." *Journal of Geography,* 49: 32–40, January 1950.

An introduction to the uses of aerial photography in studying settlement patterns, written for teachers. Includes suggestions for use, examples of interpretation, and places where photos are available.

152. Stone, Kirk H. "A Guide to Interpretation and Analysis of Aerial Photos." *American Association of Geographers, Annals,* 54: 318–328, September 1964.

A short guide to photo interpretation. Eleven topics, including transport, land use, urban features, and industry, are considered. Primarily for professional geographers but simple enough to be used as an introduction for secondary school teachers. No specific guide for study of population distribution, but the other topics noted are applicable. Most other material in the field is extremely technical.

153. Tomkins, George S. "Using the Population Map as a Point of Departure for Regional Study in the High School." *Journal of Geography,* 61: 361–363, November 1962.

Suggestions for teaching students to use and interpret maps of population distribution. Superficial, but includes some helpful ideas.

154. UNESCO. *Source Book for Geography Teaching.* New York: Longman's, 1965. 254 pp.

Methods and teaching materials in geography for primary and secondary teachers, including scattered passages on population distribution and the interrelationship of population and social and cultural variables. Presents field work techniques, methods for statistical analysis, a sample lesson outline on "The Distribution of Non-Urban Population in the Congo Basin," and a useful bibliography of sources of international statistics.

Maps, Atlases, and Aerial Photographs

155. Bruk, S. I., ed. *Atlas Narodov Mira* (*Atlas of the Peoples of the World*). Moscow: Main Administration of Geodesy and Cartography, 1964. 184 pp.

Global and regional plates show the location and density of 900 ethnic groups. The only atlas of its kind. In Russian with English translation: Telberg, V. G. *Telberg Translation to Atlas Narodov Mira.* New York: Telberg Book Corporation, 1965.

156. Burgdorfer, Friedrich, ed. *World Atlas of Population.* Hamburg: Falk-Verlag, 1954. Looseleaf, issued serially.

A collection of dot maps for major world regions, depicting topography as well as population distribution. Includes maps of smaller administrative units that do not show topographical features. Scales of regional maps range from 1: 5,000,000 to 1: 22,500,000. Small-scale auxiliary maps show population density for larger regions. Useful explanatory text and tables list density and population size. Unique collection of population maps, difficult to obtain. English and German.

157. Fullard, Harold, ed. *Philips' Modern College Atlas for Africa.* London: George Philips and Son, Ltd., 1965. 136 pp.

Sets of topical maps, for Africa and other major world regions, covering climate, vegetation, population, and economic distributions. Includes large scale plates for southern, East, and West Africa. Lack of uniformity of scale somewhat inhibits study of areal associations.

158. *Ginsburg, Norton S. *Atlas of Economic Development.* Chicago: University of Chicago Press, 1961. 119 pp. **Pa**

A series of forty-eight maps devoted to global economic distributions. Includes large scale plates for Southern, East, and West a single area or country. Ranking of each characteristic mapped by nation is helpful in analyzing association and covariance. Legend, table, and text accompanies each map. An invaluable tool.

159. *Karan, Pradyumna. "The Kingdom of Bhutan. Map Supplement No. 5." *Association of American Geographers, Annals,* 55: December 1965.

A single wall map of Bhutan, depicting settlement patterns, topography, and transportation routes. Useful tool for inferring interrelationships and areal associations (scale, 1: 253,440). Recommended for secondary school use. May be purchased from Central Office, Association of American Geographers, 1146 Sixteenth Street, N. W., Washington, D. C., 20036.

160. Miller, E. Willard. *An Economic Atlas of Pennsylvania.* Commonwealth of Pennsylvania: State Planning Board, 1964. 201 pp.

An example of the excellent materials published by state agencies. Contains ninety maps, each showing the distribution, by county, of a particular social or economic characteristic, including population, housing, manufacturing, agriculture, mining, and forests. Organization based on Ginsburg's *Atlas of Economic Development.* Invaluable visual tool for studying areal association and interrelationship of ecological factors.

161. A. J. Nystrom and Company, 3333 Elston Avenue, Chicago, Illinois 60618.

Produces a variety of regional distribution maps, several of which are comparative series. Also publishes wall maps and transparencies depicting population distribution in the United States. Puts out a fine collection of outline maps.

162. *Oxford Regional Economic Atlas, The Middle East and North Africa.* London: Oxford University Press, 1960. 135 pp.

Similar in organization to the first volume in the series, but maps with a common base are larger in scale (1: 19,000,000). Other atlases in the series, *Pakistan,* 1955, and *India and Ceylon,* 1953, include plates too small in scale to be useful.

163. *Oxford Regional Economic Atlas, U.S.S.R. and Eastern Europe.* London: Oxford University Press, 1956. 134 pp.

First volume in a series, includes sets of topical maps showing physical geography, agriculture, industry, and "human geography." The use of a common base for most maps (scale, 1: 25,000,000) facilitates comparability, but small scale detracts from effectiveness. Includes descriptive and analytical text.

164. Denoyer-Geppert Company, 5235 Ravenswood Avenue, Chicago, Illinois 60640.

Produces an excellent series of comparative distribution wall maps

72

for a number of world regions. Also publishes a complete series of wall and desk outline maps.

165. *Porter, Philip W. "East Africa-Population Distribution. Map Supplement No. 6." *Association of American Geographers, Annals,* 56: March 1966.

A well executed, wall-size population distribution map of Kenya, Uganda, and Tanzania, as of August, 1962, showing Africans, Asians, and Europeans. Listings on the reverse side show the population size and density of each country. Excellent for classroom use. May be purchased at $2.50 per copy from Central Office, Association of American Geographers, 1146 Sixteenth Street, N. W., Washington, D. C. 20036.

166. Rand McNally and Company, Education Division. Box 7600, Chicago, Illinois 60680.

This map company publishes a variety of useful maps and atlases, including an excellent series of outline maps, several of which are transparencies.

167. Sinclair, D. J., ed. *The Faber Atlas.* London: GEO Publishing Company, Ltd., 1956. 146 pp.

A collection of density and distribution maps for all major world regions. The small scale somewhat inhibits school use. Larger-scale plates of British Isles (pp. 26–20) depict distribution of population, industries and power, railways, land use, and farm types. Helpful for analyzing areal association.

168. Thrower, Norman J. W. "Annals Map Supplement Number 7. California Population Distribution in 1960." *Association of American Geographers, Annals,* 56: June 1966.

A wall map, at a scale of 1: 1,000,000, using the dot method of representation, and including topographical features. Excellent for classroom use. May be purchased at $2.50 a copy from Central Office, Association of American Geographers, 1146 Sixteenth Street, N. W., Washington, D. C. 20036.

169. Trewartha, Glenn T. "New Map of China's Population." *Geographical Review,* 47: 234–239, April 1957.

An early example of a journal article devoted to regional population distribution. Includes maps based on 1945 Chinese data and an analysis of how environmental, social, and economic factors influence distribution.

170. Trewartha, Glenn T. "New Population Maps for Uganda, Kenya, Nyasaland and Gold Coast." *Association of American Geographers, Annals,* 47: 41–58, March 1957.

Population distribution of four African political units, by one of the deans of population geography. Emphasizes clustering of native populations and stresses cultural as well as environmental factors in explaining the uneven distribution. Minority populations of Europeans, Indians, and Arabians are not considered. Dot maps. Example of the many items on regional population distribution found in geography journals.

171. U. S. Department of Commerce, Bureau of the Census. "U. S. Population Distribution, Urban and Rural: 1950." Washington: U. S. Government Printing Office, 1953.

A wall map of U. S. population distribution, using the dot method and considering as rural places of less than 2500 population. The impression of vast empty spaces mars its usefulness, but it is probably the most accessible map of its kind. May be purchased for 35¢ from Superintendent of Documents, U. S. Government Printing Office, Washington, D. C. 20401.

172. U. S. Geological Survey. Department of Interior, Washington, D. C. 20240.

This agency has large scale aerial maps and photographs for various areas in the United States which may be purchased upon request. Similar photographs may be available from agencies in other countries.

Films and Filmstrips

173. *A Look At Soviet Agriculture.* U. S. Department of Agriculture. Du Art Film Laboratories, 245 W. 55th Street, New York, New York 10015 (1959). Color. 18 minutes.

"Follows an Agricultural Economic delegation of the U. S. Department of Agriculture as it tours the farms, research stations, and other agricultural enterprises in the ten major farming regions of Russia." (EFLA)

174. *A Strand Breaks.* (The Web of Life Series). Encyclopedia Britannica Films, 1150 Wilmette Avenue, Wilmette, Illinois 60091 (1950). Color. 15 minutes.

"When the balance of nature is broken, the consequences are usually tragic. A community that has suffered destruction as a result of one element of nature getting out of balance is studied. Overgrazing and too much hunting have destroyed the grasslands and the forest." (EFLA)

175. *A Strand Grows*. (The Web of Life Series). Encyclopedia Britannica Films, 1150 Wilmette Avenue, Wilmette, Illinois 60091 (1950). Color. 15 minutes.

"A description of how living organisms work together in nature to complete nature's cycles. . . . A detailed explanation of the growth and development of a climax forest stresses the significance of a state of balance in nature, a state essential to prosperous human life." (EFLA) The steady-state of an ecosystem as demonstrated in a natural setting.

176. *Chilean Nitrate—Gift of the Desert*. Hollywood Film Enterprise, Inc., 6060 Sunset Boulevard, Hollywood, California (1947). Black and white, and color. 10 minutes.

"Visualizes the mining, refining and transportation of nitrate of soda in the Atacama desert of Northern Chile." (EFLA)

177. *Coast to Coast Geography from the Air*. United Airlines, 277 Park Avenue, New York, New York 10017. 55 frames.

A filmstrip of aerial photographs of major cities in the United States, emphasizing industrial and central business districts. Lack of detail limits its usefulness.

178. *Gold Discovery in Otago*. New Zealand Embassy, 19 Observatory Circle, N. W., Washington, D. C. 20008. Silent. 52 frames.

This filmstrip deals with the geography of New Zealand. It shows the part played by the discovery of gold in the development of Otago. It also depicts the gold rush, methods used, life of the gold rushers, and the hardships they endured. It also contains useful maps, charts, and diagrams. (Educators Guide to Free Social Studies Materials) (Note: Otago is a region south of Westland, which underwent similar changes.)

179. *The Jungle and the Plow*. UNESCO. Contemporary Films, Inc., 267 West 25 Street, New York, New York 10001 (1957). Color. 25 minutes.

"Portrays the work of a UNESCO team in Ceylon where they train villagers to improve agricultural methods and thus to increase the productivity of the area. Treats the religion of the people, geographical regions, and principal crops of the country." (EFLA)

180. *Megalopolis, Cradle of the Future.* Twentieth Century Fund Distributors. Encyclopedia Britannica Films, 1150 Wilmette Avenue, Wilmette, Illinois 60091 (1962). Black and white, and color. 20 minutes.

Description of dynamics of urbanization and concentration of population in urban nations, with narration by the noted geographer, Dr. Jean Gottman. Use of live photography and animation. (Adapted from EFLA)

181. *Nature's Way: The Inland Pond.* Welman Films, Lebanon, Connecticut 06249. Black and white, and color. 14 minutes.

"Traces the interrelationship among the animals of an inland pond, but illustrates in detail the transfer of nourishment from plant to predator. . . Valuable introduction to the ecology of a small pond." (EFLA)

182. *New Lives for Old* (Horizons of Science Series). Educational Testing Service, 20 Nassau Street, Princeton, New Jersey 08540 (1959). Color. 20 minutes.

"A case history in cultural anthropology showing the changes in the life of the Manus people of the Admiralty Islands as a result of the presence of U. S. troops during World War II. Features Dr. Margaret Mead of the American Museum of Natural History." (EFLA)

183. *Our Changing Environment.* Encyclopedia Britannica Films, 1150 Willmette Avenue, Willmette, Illinois 60091. Color. 17½ minutes.

Detailed examination of two contrasting ecosystems: a natural environment (pond) and an artificial environment (the city). Man's role in changing the ecosystem is surveyed. Problems created by man in the city and its environs and suggestions as to the elimination of these problems are discussed. (Adapted from Getis)

184. *Plant-Animal Communities: The Changing Balance of Nature.* Coronet Films, 65 E. S. Water Street, Chicago, Illinois 60601 (1963). Black and white, and color. 11 minutes.

"This film explains food chains and predator-prey relationships.

The laws of the earth are such that violation disrupts the balance of nature. The film presents a number of selected examples to prove this point. It concludes that living things must continually adjust to change." (EFLA)

185. *Population Patterns in the United States.* Coronet Films, 65 E. S. Water Street, Chicago, Illinois 60601 (1961). Black and white, and color. 11 minutes.

Traces history of growth of the westward movement in America. Points out factors affecting contemporary population growth and movement, such as changing birth and death rates, increasing life span, rural urban migration, and suburbanization. (Adapted from EFLA)

186. *Tropical Mountain Island.* United World Films, 221 Park Avenue South, New York, New York 10003 (1948). Black and white. 22 minutes.

"Close-up of Java's lands, peoples, and occupations. Begins at a seaport and follows a train journey to the mountainous area of the country, showing changes in climate, environment and industry." (EFLA)

Guides to Sources

187. Brown, James et al. *A. V. Instruction: Materials and Methods.* See No. 142.

188. *Educational Film Library Association. *Film Evaluation Guide, 1946–1964.* New Haven, Connecticut: Readers Press, 1965. 528 pp.

This extremely useful guide is a listing of recent films, providing basic information and evaluation "by an experienced group of film users," for each film. Tells how to obtain films. Excellent listing of geographical and anthropological films depicting various world regions.

189. Educational Media Council. *Educational Media Index.* Volume 12. *Geography and History.* New York: McGraw-Hill, 1964. 317 pp.

One volume of a mediocre series devoted to compilation of instructional resources. Only some entries are annotated. Includes a useful bibliography of guides to audio-visual and other instructional materials.

190. Krahn, Frederic A. *Educational Film Guide.* 11th ed. New York: The H. W. Wilson Co., 1953. Annual supplements through 1962. Discontinued.

The most comprehensive listing of educational films available. Includes a directory of places where films may be purchased, rented, or borrowed. Classified by subject.

191. Long, M., ed. *Handbook for Geography Teachers.* See No. 130.

192. Marsh, Susan. *Teaching About Maps.* See No. 145.

193. National Council of Geography Teachers. *Geographical Films* (Special Publication No. 3). National Council of Geography Teachers, 1954.

An annotated list, somewhat outdated, arranged according to country. Some films, particularly of villages and communities, will provide visual material for ecological studies.

194. Suttles, Patricia H. *Educators' Guide to Free Social Studies Materials.* 5th ed. Randolph, Wisconsin: Educators' Progress Service, 1965. 478 pp.

An annotated guide listing 1343 films, 114 free filmstrips, and 745 other free supplementary items. A source index provides a listing of the names and addresses of the organizations from which material can be obtained.

REGIONAL CASE STUDIES

The major portion of this section, Part A, is based on sample case studies from various world regions. The framework here consists of a cluster of articles introduced by a short preparatory note indicating the general theme, followed by representative annotated entries—books, articles, and visual materials—that offer data on the particular region. The studies are intended to help teachers visualize how a classroom case may be developed, to provide a framework for further studies, and to indicate the materials that may be utilized in "working up" a region for student use.

Parts B and C of this section are devoted to collected readings and individual articles that may suggest further case studies. They are, of course, only selected samples, and the teacher will also want to look into collections, general works, and journals for ideas suitable to his classes and curriculum.

A. SAMPLE CASE BIBLIOGRAPHIES

The "Virgin Lands" Program: Whither the Wheat?

In the early 1950's the Soviet government inaugurated a policy to increase the national grain output by expanding the cultivation of the "virgin" or "idle" lands in the eastern steppe region of Northern Kazakhstan and Western Siberia. The policy was regarded as risky because of the nature of the steppe soils and climate. The new program also necessitated adjustments in population distribution, agricultural technology, transport technology, manufacturing technology, and political and social organization. In many instances the adjustments were not implemented or instituted at a sufficiently rapid pace. However, a precarious balance developed, and for the first several years the grain yields increased. In 1963, a drastic reduction in grain production, caused by a series of droughts, frosts, and poor agronomic practices, upset the ecological balance. A disequilibrium was created, the results of which had regional, national, and international repercussions.

Data Limitations

Soviet and Western interpretations of the success of the "Virgin Lands" program differ markedly. Abundant statistical data are available but are of questionable reliability. Information on the grain crisis after 1963 may be obtained from current magazine and newspaper articles.

195. *Central Asian Review. (Central Asian Research Center). (1953–). Quarterly. Geoffrey Wheeler, ed. 66 King's Road, London, S. W. 3.

Includes short articles on current developments in Soviet Central Asia, "as reflected in Soviet publications." Up-to-date selections appear on all aspects of the "Virgin Lands" program including reports on population, social organization, and technology.

196. *Durgin, Frank A. "The Virgin Lands Programme, 1954–1960." Soviet Studies, 13: 255–280, January 1962.

A thorough treatment of the program through 1960, with a year-by-year progress report of grain production and an assessment of the difficulties encountered. Reports production and population data for the period.

197. Harris, Chauncy D. "U.S.S.R. Resources: Agriculture." Focus, 8, No. 5, January 1963. S

A short but incisive review of the slow progress of Soviet agriculture, allegedly caused by "the harsh physical environment" and "unfavorable human conditions." Excellent analysis of climatic conditions, with extremely useful maps.

198. *Jackson, W. A. Douglas. "The Virgin and Idle Lands of Western Siberia and Northern Kazakhstan: A Geographical Appraisal." *Geographical Review*, 46: 1–19, January 1966.

An appraisal of the possibilities of expanding Soviet wheat production, noting the marginal nature of Soviet agriculture, the organizational problems, and the climatic and soil conditions. Includes excellent maps of the region.

199. *Jackson, W. A. Douglas. "The Virgin and Idle Lands Program Reappraised." *Association of American Geographers, Annals*, 52: 69–79, March 1962.

An evaluation of the Soviet agricultural expansion program for the eastern steppe region. Notes the climatic, soil, organizational, and technological problems that caused the program to meet with only limited success.

200. Karcz, Jerzy F. and V. P. Timoshenko. "Soviet Agricultural Policy, 1953–1962." *Food Research Institute Studies*, 4: 123–164, 1963–1964.

The emphasis here is on the political aspect of the program. See especially the postscript for an analysis of the grain crisis of 1963. Includes statistical charts and tables.

201. Lewis, Robert A. "The Irrigation Potential of Soviet Central Asia." *Annals of the Association of American Geographers*, 52: 99–114, March 1962.

A scholarly evaluation of the difficulties inherent in the expansion of Central Asian irrigation. Further expansion beyond present plans involves very much more costly investment.

202. Lydolph, Paul E. *Geography of the U.S.S.R.* New York: John Wiley and Sons, 1964. 451 pp.

See Chapter 11, "Western Siberia and Northern Kazakhstan," for a short analysis of the physical setting, agriculture, and population of the "Virgin Lands" region. This recent regional geography includes excellent maps.

203. Mellor, Roy E. H. *Geography of the U.S.S.R.* New York: St. Martin's Press, 1965. 403 pp.

A recent geography, with a topical approach, including chapters on "The Physical Environment of Russia," "Climate, Soils, and Vegetation," and "The Geography of Agriculture."

204. Olson, Eugene T. "The New Soviet Lands—Destiny or Dust." *Foreign Agriculture*, 25: 4–6, February 1961.

A discussion of the problems confronting the "Virgin Lands" program, with an analysis of possible effects on the land and on crop production. Includes a map delimiting the region.

The Village Marshmen of Southern Iraq

A study of an apparently static society, adapted to the unique environment of the Lower Tigris and Euphrates, with an economy based on reed gathering and buffalo herding. Only recently have political and economic intrusions threatened to upset the society of the sedentary marsh Arabs, whose distinct tribal loyalties are creating a "social psychological" resistance.

Data Limitations

Population statistics are minimal, and much of the accessible material is based on the observations of one writer.

205. Cressey, George B. *Crossroads: Land and Life in Southwest Asia.* Chicago: J. B. Lippincott, 1960. 593 pp.

A general human geography, with both a topical and regional analysis. Includes extensive bibliographies and a useful chapter on Iraq.

206. Harris, George L. *Iraq: Its People, Its Society, Its Culture* (Survey of World Cultures). New Haven: Human Relations Area Files Press, 1958. 350 pp. **S**

An excellent overview of Iraq, stressing societal interrelationships, and focusing on change. May be read by high school students.

207. Jacobsen, Thorkild and Robert M. Adams. "Salt and Silt in Ancient Mesopotamian Agriculture." *Science,* 128: 1251–1257, November 21, 1958. **B-M Reprint G–105**

The agricultural technology of an ancient culture contributed to salinity and silting problems which, in turn, contributed to the breakup of the civilization itself.

208. Salim. S. M. *Marsh Dwellers of the Euphrates Delta* (London

School of Economics Monographs on Social Anthropology No. 23). London: University of London, Athlone Press, 1962. 157 pp.

A thorough, well organized anthropological study of a group of marsh dwellers who have already been affected by the "outside." In this study in depth of one village, the author pays particular attention to the effect of political and economic changes upon the structure of marsh society, and emphasizes the role of tribal values and obligations in the changing ecosystem. Includes demographic material.

209. Thesiger, Wilfred. *The Marsh Arabs.* New York: E. P. Dutton, 1964. 241 pp. S

A simply written and easily comprehensible work describing the author's travels through the marshlands in the 1950's. The volume is often rambling and unscholarly, but includes comments on all aspects of marsh life.

210. Thesiger, Wilfred. "Marsh Dwellers of Southern Iraq." *National Geographic Magazine,* 113: 205–239, February, 1958. S

A flowery, melodramatic text, saved by some excellent photography. Emphasis on Ma'dan technical skill, transport, and social organization.

211. Thesiger, Wilfred. "The Marshmen of Southern Iraq." *Geographical Journal,* 120: 272–281, September 1954.

A primary account of the Ma'dan marshmen, emphasizing environment, technology and economic organization.

The Effect of the "Culture System" on the Island of Java, 1830–1869

Before the colonial period in Netherlands India, there was a fairly well set ecological pattern in Java, characterized by a cooperative traditional society, intensive wet-rice agriculture, and powerful village law (*adat*). In 1830 the Dutch government introduced the "culture system," a politico-economic policy established to increase peasant agricultural production and Dutch profits. This colonial policy was most upsetting to the equilibrium on Java. Changes took place in population, social and political organization, and agricultural technology. Some argue that Indonesia's population problem today stems in part from the impact of the "culture system."

Data Limitations

Discrepancies in the literature over the true effect of the system create problems for a study of this kind. However, many challenging questions are raised as well. Limited material is available on village social organization before the introduction of the system.

212. Broek, Jan O. M. "Indonesia." *Focus*, 7, No. 4, December 1956. S

A general survey of the environment, peoples, agriculture, resources, and vegetation in this crisis-ridden nation. The excellent maps are by Vincent Kotschar.

213. Broek, Jan O. M. *Indonesia* (American Geographical Society around The World Program). Garden City, New York: Nelson Doubleday, 1962. 63 pp. S

General picture of the diversity of Indonesia, including data on peoples, environment, history, and economy. JHS.

214. Furnivall, J. S. *Colonial Policy and Practice: A Comparative Study Of Burman and Netherlands India.* New York: New York University Press, 1956. 568 pp.

————. *Netherlands India: A Study of A Plural Economy.* Cambridge: Cambridge University Press, 1939. 502 pp.

Two well respected works on Dutch colonial policy. Include detailed analyses of the theory, nature and consequences of the "culture system."

215. Geertz, Clifford. *Agricultural Involution; The Process of Ecological Change in Indonesia.* Berkeley: University of California Press, 1963. 176 pp.

In this unique volume an anthropologist examines the interrelationship of wet-rice agriculture, colonial policy, and population change, in an effort to evaluate the problems of contemporary Indonesian economic development. Analyzes the "culture system" in this context. Includes an excellent introduction, explaining the nature of ecosystems and the approach of cultural ecology. Some times obscure, but thoughtful and well integrated.

216. *Higgins, Benjamin and Jean Higgins. *Indonesia: The Crisis of the Millstones.* Princeton, New Jersey: D. Van Nostrand, 1963. 144 pp. Pa

Another of the excellent regional studies in the Van Nostrand

Searchlight Series. Examines clearly and succinctly the resources, climate, economy, and politics in contemporary Indonesia. See especially Chapter 5, "The Economic History." Well written, accessible, and compact.

217. Legge, J. P. *Indonesia.* Englewood Cliffs, New Jersey: 1964. 184 pp. **Pa S**

Palmier, Leslie. *Indonesia.* New York: Walker and Co., 1965. 240 pp. **S**

Two recent publications analyze contemporary Indonesia from a historical perspective. Sources of general information, with summary material on the period of the "culture system." Easy reading.

218. Wertheim, W. T. *Indonesian Society in Transition; A Study of Social Change.* The Hague: W. Van Hoeve, Ltd., 1956. 360 pp.

Focuses on twentieth-century social history, but includes useful descriptions of pre-European society and nineteenth-century developments. See relevant sections in the following chapters: 6, "The Changing Status System"; 9, "The Changing Pattern of Labor Relations"; and 10, "Cultural Dynamics in Indonesia."

The Chilean Nitrate Industry: A Study in Changing Resource Use

Sodium nitrate was present in the Atacama desert before the late nineteenth century, but it was not perceived or developed as a "resource" until its uses were discovered, and mining and transportation technology made its extraction profitable. The development of the nitrate industry transformed the Atacama desert and the entire Northern Region: rail lines were built, pipelines laid, ports developed, settlement boomed, population grew, and the landscape was changed. By the 1920's, the nature of sodium nitrate as a resource was changing. The European development of synthetic fertilizers and the extraction of nitrogen from the air made the Chilean nitrate industry unprofitable and led to readjustments in the entire system. A new technology changed the face of an entire region.

Data Limitations

Material is scant on the mine workers because of the transient nature of many of the settlements. Numerous publications are in Spanish and French. Primary statistics are in Spanish, although some English summaries exist. See especially: *Boletin de la Sociedad nacional de minería;* Ministerio de Economía y Comercio, Secretaría General de Censo, *Censo Económico nacional; Revista Geográfica de Chile;* Dirección general de estadistica, *Estadistica chileña,* Santiago de Chile.

219. Allen, A. W. "South America's Leading Mining Industry—Nitrate." *Engineering and Mining Journal,* 126: 816–824, November 24, 1928.

An extremely optimistic view of the future of the Chilean nitrate industry written just before its collapse. Provides information on geology, climate, and technology. Excellent pictures.

220. Bascunan, Arturo. "The Nitrate Industry in Chile." *Canadian Geographical Journal,* 18: 17–25, February 1939.

A short but useful article describing the cultural development of the nitrate region, its location, land forms, and modern extraction processes.

221. Bowen, J. David. *The Land and People of Chile* (Portrait of the Nations Series). Philadelphia: J. B. Lippincott, 1966. 154 pp. S

Hanson, Earl Parker. *Chile* (American Geographical Society Around the World Program). Garden City, New York: Nelson Doubleday, 1958. 64 pp. S

Both volumes provide easy reading, pictures, maps, and useful general information.

222. *Bowman, Isiah. *Desert Trails of the Atacama* (American Geographical Society, Special Publication No. 5). New York: A. G. S., 1924. 362 pp.

*Rudolph, William E. *Vanishing Trails of Atacama* (American Geographical Society, Research Series No. 24). New York: A. G. S., 1963. 87 pp.

Two surveys of the Atacama desert region, written fifty years apart. Bowman's classic work contains a wealth of information, with particularly useful sections on the population of the "nitrate desert." Rudolph assesses the changes in the region since Bowman's original visit. Valuable sources.

223. "From the Chilean Desert: Life-Giving Nitrate, One of the Nation's Top Exports." *Américas,* 8: 25–28, June 1956.

A short history of the changes in the organization and technology of the Chilean nitrate industry.

224. James, Preston E. *Latin America.* 3rd ed. New York: Odyssey Press, 1959. 942 pp.

The standard text on Latin-American geography, with a historical-cultural orientation. Excellent general overview of the region.

225. Pan American Union. *Nitrate Fields of Chile* (Commodities of Commerce Series No. 11). 4th ed. Washington, D. C., 1935.

Concerned with the modernization and change in organization of the industry since the development of synthetic nitrates.

226. Rich, John L. "The Nitrate District of Tarápaca, Chile: An Aerial Traverse." *Geographical Review,* 31: 1–22, January 1941.

A series of twenty-two aerial photographs showing the geology, geography, and cultural phenomena associated with the Chilean nitrate industry. The accompanying text describes changes in technology since the discovery of extraction of nitrogen from the air.

227. Rudolph, W. E. "Chile." *Focus,* 7, No. 9, May 1957. **S**

A summary of the contemporary economic status of Chile, with superb maps and a short note on nitrates.

228. Whitbeck, R. H. "Chilean Nitrate and the Nitrogen Revolution." *Economic Geography,* 7: 273–283, July 1931.

An illuminating article, emphasizing the effect of the new nitrogen technology on Chile. Also includes sections on location, origin, and geology of the deposits.

The Valley of Central Mexico: The Aztecs and the Spanish Conquest

A bibliography for studying the impact of the Spanish conquistadors upon the Aztec-dominated Valley of central Mexico. An extended description of the case is found in Chapter 1.

229. Cook, Sherburne and Simpson, Lesley B. *The Population of Central Mexico in the Sixteenth Century* (Ibero-Americana No. 31). Berkeley: University of California Press, 1948. 241 pp.

". . . Population density and distribution in one of Latin America's major zones of human occupance, past or present, has been reconstructed through contemporary documents and a consideration of changing soil characteristics." (Church)

230. Diaz del Castillo, Bernal. *The Discovery and Conquest of Mexico.* New York: Grove Press, 1956. 478 pp. **Pa**

A personal record of the Spanish conquest, with scattered first-hand observations of the environment, social organization, technology, and population of Tenochtitlán. More a narration of conquest and travels than an observation of the society and culture.

231. Fox, David J. "Water Problems of the Aztec Capital (Mexico City)." *The Geographical Magazine,* 40: 468–479, October 1967.

A report on the many far-reaching hydraulic and health problems produced by the intervention of the Spaniards in the Valley of Central Mexico.

232. *Gibson, Charles. *The Aztecs under Spanish Rule: A History of the Indians of the Valley of Mexico, 1519–1810.* Stanford, California: Stanford University Press, 1964. 657 pp.

Concentrates on the organizational, environmental, technological, and population changes which took place in the Valley of Mexico following the Spanish conquest. Includes a chapter devoted to changes in the city.

233. Long, John E. *Mexico* (American Geographical Society around the World Program). Garden City, New York: Nelson Doubleday, Inc., 1955. 63 pp. **S**

An overview of contemporary Mexico, with some historical passages. Written for the secondary school student.

234. Millon, Rene. "Teotihuacán." *Scientific American,* 216: 38–48, June 1967.

A searching and readable article on the pre-Aztec city of Teotihuacán, written from an archaeological point of view, yet casting much light upon pre-Columbian urban ecology in the Valley of Central Mexico. The city studied was highly organized and was larger in area than imperial Rome.

235. "Mexico." *Focus,* 15, June 1966. **S**

A short portrait of the landscape, climate, population, and culture of modern Mexico. Excellent for a general orientation, with maps.

236. *Prescott, William H. *History of the Conquest of Mexico.* New York: Modern Library. 863 pp.

A classic history, including extensive, well written material on all aspects of Aztec civilization prior to conquest (see Book I), and a discussion of the changes brought about by the conquest. A necessary source.

237. *Vaillant, George C. *The Aztecs of Mexico.* Garden City, New York: Doubleday, Doran and Co., 1941. 340 pp. **S**

A classic history of the Indians of the Valley of Mexico, including extensive information on the environment, organization, and technology of the Aztec people of Mexico City (Tenochtitlán). Two chapters are devoted to changes brought about by the Spanish conquest. Extensive bibliography. Portions appropriate for secondary school students.

238. Von Hagen, Victor W. *The Aztec: Man and Tribe.* New York: The New American Library, 1958. 222 pp. **Pa S**

An archeological history, for the general reader, including much information on the environment, political and social organization, religion, and technology of the people of Tenochtitlán. Excellent drawings.

The Pagan Hill Folk of Jos Plateau

The pagan tribes of Northern Nigeria were forced to settle in the hills when their stronger neighbors, the Hausa and Fulani, engaged in slave raiding and holy wars. The hill folk had developed an ingenious agricultural technology, based on terraced farming, that supported a dense population in a limited environment. In the early twentieth century, cessation of the slave raids, introduction of tin mining into the area, and governmental resettlement schemes contributed to upset the ecological equilibrium of the hill folk communities. Today, profound changes are visible in the population distribution, technology, and social and economic organization of these once isolated tribes.

239. *Buchanan, K. M. and J. C. Pugh. *Land and People in Nigeria.* London: University of London Press, 1955. 252 pp.

The basic human geography for Nigeria, emphasizing environmental setting, resources and industry and settlement patterns. See pp. 109–111 for a discussion of terraced farming. Original maps and diagrams.

240. Floyd, Barry. "The Federal Republic of Nigeria." *Focus*, 15: October 1964. **S**

Mitchel, N. C. "Nigeria." *Focus*, 4: March 1954. **S**

General summaries of the Nigerian environment, culture, resources, and political and social organization; one article written before independence and one after. Easy reading.

241. Gleave, Michael B. "The Changing Frontiers of Settlement in the Uplands of Northern Nigeria." *The Nigerian Geographical Journal*, 8: 127–141, December 1965.

A survey of various tribes on the plateau, emphasizing changes in technology and economic organization and describing the re-advance of the population into the plains.

242. Grove, A. T. *Land Use and Soil Conservation on the Jos Plateau.* Nigeria: Geological Survey, Bulletin No. 22, 1952. 63 pp.

Rich source for land form, climatic, soil, and resource data. Describes native technology and social organization, with a colonial bias. Includes land use map and 1945–1946 population statistics.

243. Hance, William. *The Geography of Modern Africa.* New York: Columbia University Press, 1964. 653 pp.

The best standard economic geography of Africa, with a regional-topical organization. Teachers.

244. Irons, Evelyn. *Nigeria* (American Geographical Society around the World Program). Garden City, New York: Nelson Doubleday, Inc., 1966. 64 pp. S

Excellent for a general orientation to modern Nigeria. JHS students.

245. Kennedy, J. D. "The Jos Plateau: Its People and Some Aspects of Forestry." *The Empire Forestry Review*, 28: 152–161, June 1949.

Useful for its data on the land forms, climate, soils, and biotic and mineral resources of the Jos Plateau. Some short and prejudicial comments on the hill folk are included. Teachers.

246. Kenworthy, Leonard S. *Profile of Nigeria.* Garden City, New York: Doubleday and Co., Inc., 1960. 96 pp. S

A general geography, including maps and pictures, suitable for slow learners.

247. Kimble, George H. T. *Tropical Africa.* 2 vols. New York: Twentieth Century Fund, 1960.

A survey with a geographical orientation, broad in scope, and written during a period of extreme flux. Reads easily. An important basic source for African economic and social conditions.

248. Miller, Ronald. "Cultivation of Terraces in Nigeria." *The Geographical Journal,* 118: 110–111, 1952.

A short note on the development of terrace farming, noteworthy because of its reference to sentiment (social psychology) as a factor in the changing hill folk ecosystem.

249. *Netting, Robert M. "Heritage of Survival." *Natural History,* 74: 14–21, March 1965.

A description of the agricultural technology of the Kofyar terrace farmers of the Jos Plateau. Includes material on land form, climate, and social and economic organization. Also analyzes the effect of the cessation of warfare and slave raiding on the community. Rich source with excellent photographs.

The Ceylon Dry Zone in Ancient Times

From approximately the 4th century B.C. to the 13th century A.D., there existed in the Dry Zone of Ceylon a highly structured village-dwelling society with a well developed irrigation technology and a strong central government, supporting a presumably large population. In the 13th century, outside invasions and the ensuing onset of malaria are thought to have caused the decline and eventual disappearance of this once great society.

Data Limitations

Abundant material is available for all factors, but discrepancies exist relating to the causes of the decline. This raises interesting questions, however. Population data exist, but are of uncertain validity.

250. Arusaratnam, S. *Ceylon.* Englewood Cliffs, New Jersey: Prentice-Hall, 1963. 182 pp. **S**

A recent work, with an excellent section concentrating on the social and political organization and the irrigation technology of classical Ceylon, from 200 B.C. to 1200 A.D. See especially "Decline and Decadence, A.D. 1200–1500." A bibliographic essay evaluates the major relevant works. Highly readable.

251. Boltin, Lee. *Ceylon* (American Geographical Society around the World Series). Garden City, New York: Nelson Doubleday, 1961. 64 pp. **S**

An excellent introduction for students to the contemporary and historical features of Ceylonese society. Highly recommended for basic background material.

252. *Ceylon Historical Journal.* (1951–   ). Quarterly. 129 Dutugemunu Street, Dehiwela, Ceylon.

   The Ceylon Journal of Historical and Social Studies. (1958–   ). Bi-Annual. University of Ceylon, Peradeniya.

   These scholarly journals publish detailed essays, by experts, on various aspects of ancient and medieval society.

253. De Silva, S. F. "A Geographical Interpretation of Ceylon History." *Bulletin of the Ceylon Geographical Society,* 9: 44–58, July-December 1955. **S**

   A somewhat oversimplified study, with an emphasis on the influence of geography upon history, but not a purely deterministic approach. Part IV includes a short history of the ancient irrigation period, with reference to geographical conditions and social organization. Suitable reading level for HS students.

254. *Geiger, William. *The Culture of Ceylon in Medieval Times.* Heinz Bechert, ed. Wiesbaden: Otto Harrassowitz, 1960. 286 pp.

   A thorough treatment of Sinhalese culture, from the 4th to 15th centuries A.D., by an expert in oriental studies. Includes detailed analyses of environment; economic, political, and social organization; technology. A rich source, referring to significant works.

255. *Ginsburg, Norton, ed. *The Pattern of Asia.* Englewood Cliffs, New Jersey: Prentice-Hall, 1958, 927 pp.

   A vast but clear and informative geography, written by regional experts and aimed at "a more basic understanding of the processes of change which are radically transforming the Asian landscape" (Ginsburg). An authoritative work, with invaluable bibliographical notes and comments.

256. von der Lippe, Paul. "Ceylon Restores Its Ancient Irrigation Works." *Civil Engineering,* 21: 41–44, September 1951.

   A brief description of Ceylon's ancient irrigation works, with useful material on the technology of the period.

257. *Murphey, Rhoads. "The Ruin of Ancient Ceylon." *The Journal of Asian Studies,* 16: 181–200, February 1957. **B-M Reprint G–167**

A noted Asian geographer describes the environment, technology, and organization of the dry zone in ancient times, and discusses the factors which may have contributed to the decline of that society. A most perceptive and analytical article, with important bibliographical notes. An excellent framework for a study and a good starting place.

258. Wikkramatileke, Rudolf. *Southeast Ceylon: Trends and Problems in Agricultural Settlement* (University of Chicago, Department of Geography, Research Paper No. 83). Chicago: University of Chicago Press, 1963. 163 pp.

A study of contemporary agriculture in a portion of the dry zone. Includes comprehensive soil, climate, resource, and land form data for the area. For our purposes, see Chapter III, "The Historical Background," which includes material on ancient organization and population. Includes maps and photographs.

THE "GOLDEN AGE" IN NORTH WESTLAND, NEW ZEALAND

For many centuries this West Coast area of the South Island of New Zealand was occupied by a small number of hunter-gatherer Maoris. In the middle of the nineteenth century extractive industry was introduced into the region. With the discovery of gold came drastic changes in the landscape, population, and economic, social, and political organization. Few aspects of this relatively uninhabited area remained unchanged.

Today, the West Coast is considered a "problem area." A further investigation might lead students to develop a second case study, centered upon the decline of the region and the emergence of new interrelationships.

Data Limitations

Abundant material is available, but McCaskill's work is relied upon because it is most accessible and professional. Demographic material abounds.

259. Clark, Andrew Hill. *The Invasion of New Zealand by People, Plants and Animals* (Rutgers University Studies in Geography No. 1). New Brunswick, New Jersey: Rutgers University Press, 1949. 465 pp.

An historical geography of the South Island, considering the effect of people, "plants and animals, and potatoes and pigs" on the pre-European habitat. Useful survey of landform, climate and vegetation. The extensive bibliography includes primary sources applicable to this study.

260. Cumberland, K. B. "Moas and Men: New Zealand about A.D. 1250." *Geographical Review,* 52: 151–173, April 1962. **B-M Reprint G–44**

An excellent analysis of the man-environment interconnections which developed as a result of the destructive moa-hunting economy. A classic case of dysfunctional environmental modification arising from an exploitative economy.

261. Gibbs, H. S. and A. D. Mercer. "Soils and Agriculture of Westland New Zealand." *Soil Bureau Bulletin No. 2.* Wellington, 1950. 24 pp.

A prime example of the type of government publication so useful in compiling data. Notes topography, geology, and climate as well as agriculture and soil. Includes large scale soil maps.

262. Hargreaves, R. P. "The Golden Age: New Zealand about 1867." *New Zealand Geographer,* 16: 1–32, April 1960.

General historical geography of the period, with sections on gold mining on the West Coast.

263. Laubenfels, David J. "New Zealand." *Focus,* 11: September 1960. **S**

A survey of the eight dominant landscapes of New Zealand, with a short economic analysis. Includes an excellent set of maps.

264. McCaskill, Murray. "The Course of Settlement in Westland." *Proceedings of the Third New Zealand Geography Conference.* New Zealand Geographical Society, 1962, pp. 79–84.

A short but significant essay, enumerating changes in each of three phases of settlement in the second half of the nineteenth century. Excellent tables summarize population change.

265. *McCaskill, Murray. "Man and Landscape in North Westland New Zealand." S. R. Eyre and G. R. J. Jones, eds. *Geography as Human Ecology; Methodology by Example.* New York: St. Martin's Press, 1966, pp. 264–290.

Should be used as the basic framework for the case. Not only covers the basic data, but keenly analyzes the changing inter-relationships of man and land. A good starting point.

266. McCaskill, Murray. *New Zealand* (Longmans Australian Geographies, No. 21). Victoria, Australia: Longmans, Green and Co., Ltd. 40 pp. **S**

Pownall, L. L. *New Zealand* (American Geographical Society Around the World Program). Garden City, New York: Nelson Doubleday, 1964. 64 pp. **S**

Two simply written economic and physical geographies for students, including general material on landscape, climate, and resources. Both volumes have useful maps and photographs.

267. McCaskill, Murray. "The Poutini Coast: A Geography of Maori Settlement in Westland." *New Zealand Geographer,* 10: 134–150, October 1954.

The human geography of Westland inhabitants in the mid-nineteenth century, before European settlement. Includes data on environment, economic and social organization, and population. A "setting" for the study. Good bibliography.

268. McCaskill, Murray. "The South Island Goldfields in the 1860's: Some Geographical Aspects." Murray McCaskill, ed. *Land and Livelihood: Geographical Essays in Honor of George Jobberns.* New Zealand Geographical Society: Miscellaneous series No. 4, 1962, pp. 143–169.

A consideration of the spread of settlement, population patterns, physical environment, and mining techniques of the Westland and Otago gold fields, during the first part of the "golden era." See footnotes for references to further population data.

B. COLLECTED CASE STUDIES

269. Brunhes, Jean. *Human Geography.* See No. 30.

270. Dickinson, Robert E. *City and Region.* See No. 69.

271. Eyre, S. R. and G. R. J. Jones. *Geography as Human Ecology.* See No. 2.

272. *Highsmith, Richard M., ed. *Case Studies in World Geography.* Englewood Cliffs, New Jersey: Prentice-Hall, 1961. 218 pp. **Pa**

A series of twenty-nine short case studies, representing various geographical approaches to the relationship between man and environment, and organized according to occupance and economy type. Covers a variety of small regions and provides some ecellent material for the development of class case studies.

273. Scientific American. *Cities.* See No. 83.

274. Theodorson, George A., ed. *Studies in Human Ecology.* See No. 14.

275. Thomas, William L., ed. *Man's Role in Changing the Face of the Earth.* See No. 23.

C. INDIVIDUAL CASE STUDY IDEAS

276. Adams, Robert M. "The Origin of Cities." See No. 64.

277. Bogue, Donald J. "The Geography of Recent Population Trends in the United States." *Association of American Geographers, Annals,* 44: 124–134, June 1954.

Summary of findings presented in detail in two monographs by the author. Outline of ten national trends, with special emphasis on regional differences. Descriptive and rather truncated, but good "quickie" summary.

278. Braidwood, Robert J. "The Agricultural Revolution." *Scientific American,* 203, September 1960. **SA–605**

The rise of agricultural surpluses liberated human energy for new achievements in technology, which, in turn, further increased surpluses. This regenerative cycle of adaptations ultimately led to a complete transformation of human society.

279. Budowski, Gerard. "Tropical Savannas, a Sequence of Forest Felling and Repeated Burnings." *Turrialba,* 623–633, 1956. **B-M Reprint G–29**

A valuable paper which shows that the so-called "natural" tropical savannas of Africa and the Americas are actually produced by the uses of human culture. Another example of man *modifying* the environment as much as he adapts to it.

280. Calhoun, John B. "Population Density and Social Pathology." *Scientific American,* 206: 139–148, February 1962. **SA–506**

This seminal article explores the role of crowding on a population of Norway rats in disrupting the social organization, behavior patterns, and consequently the equilibrium of population in the colony. *Even though food is kept abundant,* the population is affected, implying that Malthusian concepts are insufficient even for animal ecological systems.

281. Caplow, Theodore. "The Social Ecology of Guatemala City." George Theodorson, ed. *Studies in Human Ecology.* Evanston, Illinois: Row Peterson and Co., 1961, pp. 331–348.

A study of the spatial distributions of a Latin American city, with a comparison to North American city structure. Social organizational and economic variables are considered, with an emphasis on culture.

282. Childe, V. Gordon. *Man Makes Himself.* New York: The New American Library of World Literature, 1951. 191 pp. **Pa S**

An eminent British anthropologist tells how man's technological ingenuity changed human culture, including population size, distribution, composition, and social organization. Emphasis on the technological "revolutions" of ancient times; of particular interest is Chapter VII, "The Urban Revolution." Considers all aspects of the ecological complex. A superb work, simple and exciting, highly recommended for HS use.

283. Crane, Robert I. "Urbanism in India." *American Journal of Sociology,* 60: 463–470, March 1965.

Descriptive historical study of urban life in India, with little emphasis on reasons for urban growth and much preoccupation with "vital processes." Of particular interest is the section devoted to trends in rural-urban migration and the "floating " population (pp. 466–67). Some space devoted to a description of the spatial distribution and structure of city populations at different points in India's history. Map of urban population distribution, 1955 (p. 455).

284. Cressey, Paul F. "Population Succession in Chicago: 1898–1930." *American Journal of Sociology,* 44: 59–69, July 1938. **B-M Reprint S–364**

A human ecologist explains the invasion-succession cycle, using Chicago as a case in point. The rapid changes in population distribution and the migratory trends of various cultural and economic groups are cited.

285. *Daedalus.* "Historical Population Studies." American Academy of Arts and Sciences, Spring 1968.

A brilliant issue of an outstanding journal, devoted entirely to population studies. Case studies of topics selected from all portions of Europe, and from Japan, and distributed in time as well as in space. The Plague in France (1720–1722), for example, is dealt with in an article by Jean-Noel Biraben. Only $1.75: a must.

286. *Deasy, George F. and Phyllis R. Griess. "Effects of a Declining Mining Economy on the Pennsylvania Anthracite Region." *American Association of Geographers, Annals,* 55: 239–259, June 1965.

Discussion of the economic and demographic effects of an industrial decline, brought about by a changing technology. Material may be adapted for a regional case study, along with the article by Willard E. Miller cited below.

287. Dotson, Floyd and Lillian Ota Dotson. "Ecological Trends in the City of Guadalajara, Mexico." *Social Forces,* 32: 367–374, May 1954. **S**

How rapid population growth and industrial development brought about changes in the ecological structure of this Mexican city. Environmental, economic, cultural, and technological variables are considered. Excellent description of spatial distribution of population and activities.

288. Eberhard, Wolfram. "Data on the Structure of the Chinese City in the Preindustrial Period." *Economic Development and Cultural Change,* 4: 253–268, April 1956.

Extremely useful historical study of the "pre-industrial" city in China. Discusses the movement, mix, and spatial distribution of city populations in a number of dynastic periods. Easily adaptable for high school students. Wealth of descriptive material.

289. Gilmore, Harlan W. "The Old New Orleans and the New: A Case for Ecology." *American Sociological Review,* 9: 385–394, 1944.

A study of the evolution of patterns of ethnic distribution in New Orleans. Environmental and topographical features are stressed as factors influencing distribution in the "old" New Orleans, while modern drainage systems and transportation developments are considered as influential factors in the spatial patterns of the "new" New Orleans. Considers cultural and organizational variables as well. Makes an interesting case study of an unusual American community.

290. Gist, Noel P. "Developing Patterns of Urban Decentralization." See No. 72.

291. Gist, Noel P. "The Ecology of Bangalore, India: An East-West Comparison." *Social Forces*, 25: 356–365, May 1957.

An effort to prove that non-Western cities do not necessarily conform to the ecological pattern of their Western counterparts, with discussion of business and industrial distribution, residential segregation and decentralization. Cultural and social factors are stressed as they influence the ecological pattern of Bangalore. Good case study of preindustrial city structure. Adaptable for high school use.

292. Gottman, Jean. "Why the Skyscraper?" *Geographical Review*, 56: 190–212, April 1966. **S**

An eminent French geographer tells how technological, economic, and organizational factors influenced the development of the skyscraper, and how in turn, the skyscraper influenced the structure of society. Relevant to the study of urban population concentration. Dr. Gottman's lucid style makes easy reading for high school students.

293. Gregor, Howard T. "Spatial Disharmonies in California Population Growth." *Geographical Review*, 53: 100–122, January 1963.

Discussion of the unique patterning of the population in California, with special reference to clustering in dry and urban coastal areas and to "urban sprawl" in metropolitan areas. The analysis of the state's population growth and distribution considers the influence of technological, social, and cultural factors.

294. *Hansen, Asael T. "The Ecology of a Latin American City." E. B. Reuter, ed. *Race and Culture Contacts*. New York: McGraw-Hill Book Company, Inc., 1934, pp. 124–142. **S**

How factors of social psychology, technology, economics, and social organization contributed to the changing spatial distribution of population in a Mexican city. Excellent case study, well suited to high school students, considering the interrelationship of all five ecological factors.

295. Harris, Marvin. "The Cultural Ecology of India's Sacred Cattle." *Current Anthropology*, 7: 51–66, February 1966.

An anthropologist looks at the relationship between the human and cattle populations in India, considering present environmental, technical, and socio-cultural conditions. Views cattle as a vital part of an ecosystem, rather than as a "useless sector of the national price market." A unique but somewhat technical study. Example of an anthropological approach to ecology.

296. Hart, John F. "The Changing Distribution of the American Negro." *Association of American Geographers, Annals,* 50: 242–266, September 1960.

Exploration of the major growth trends, changes in distribution and migration patterns. Concentrates on general trends and does not consider economic or social subgroups. Almost totally descriptive. Rich source of material for student analysis, including graphs and maps for JHS or SHS.

297. Hayner, Norman S. "Mexico City: Its Growth and Configuration." *American Journal of Sociology,* 50: 295–304, January 1945.

A historical-ecological study of the developing spatial pattern of Mexico City, emphasizing the trend toward North American zonal arrangement. Cultural, economic, social, and historical factors are considered as variables contributing to the trend. May be adapted as a case study for high school use.

298. Isaac, Erich. "On the Domestication of Cattle." *Science,* 137: 195–204, July 1962. **B-M Reprint G–98**

An interesting and challenging thesis to the effect that the domestication of cattle arose from a religious rather than an economic motivation.

299. *Langer, William S. "The Black Death." *Scientific American,* 210: 114–121, February 1964. **SA–619**

A fascinating, unique account of the effect of the epidemic of plague in fourteenth-century Europe. Traces the changes in social organization, population size and distribution, political and economic organization, and moral and religious outlook that occurred as the result of the "Great Dying."

300. Lowenthal, David and Lambros Comitas. "Emigration and Depopulation." *Geographical Review,* 52: 195–210, April 1962.

Presentation of case studies analyzing the impact of depopulation on Ithaca in Greece and Monserrat in the British West Indies. Demonstrates how population changes affect social and economic structures.

301. Mabogunje, Akin. "The Growth of Residential Districts in Ibadan." *Geographical Review,* 52: 56–77, January 1962.

Study of the changing patterns of population distribution and spatial structure in a Nigerian City. Technological, environmental, and cultural factors are considered as factors influencing change. Adaptable for use as a case study.

302. *Mencher, Joan P. "Kerala and Madras: A Comparative Study of Ecology and Social Structure." *Ethnology*, 5: 135–171, April 1961.

How ecological factors (regional topography, settlement patterns, land use, and agricultural practices) interact to produce different social and cultural institutions in two regions in southern India. Filled with fascinating examples of the complex interaction between ecology and social structure. Difficult, technical article due to use of anthropological terminology, but highly recommended to teachers with some background in the discipline. Many references to the relationship between population distribution and other variables. Excellent diagrams.

303. *Miller, E. Willard. "The Southern Anthracite Region: A Problem Area." *Economic Geography*, 31: 331–350, October 1955.

How changes in technology and resource use profoundly affected the population, economy, and social organization of a coal producing region. Portions may be adapted and used as a case study, demonstrating the dynamic interrelationship of population, technology, natural resources, and social organization.

304. Mukerjee, Radhakamal. "Ways of Dwelling in the Communities of India." George A. Theodorson, ed. *Studies in Human Ecology.* Evanston, Illinois: Row Peterson and Company, 1961, pp. 390–401.

A well written description of village, town, and city life in India, with an ecological orientation. How religious and cultural values and industrial growth contribute to the changing social and ecological patterns in these regions. For a short but noteworthy case, see the study of the village farmer (*char*), p. 392.

305. Nelson, Howard J. "Spread of an Artificial Landscape over Southern California." *Association of American Geographers, Annals,* 49: Part II, 80–99, September 1959. **B-M Reprint G–168**

Study of the recent spurt in urban growth in this region, with particular reference to industry and population. Considers factors contributing to the expansion and stresses the role of the automobile. May be modified and used as a case study for high school. Includes aerial photographs.

306. Scaff, Alvin H. "Cultural Factors in Ecological Change on Min-

danao in the Philippines." *Social Forces,* 27: 119–123, December 1948. **S**

A reaction to the classical school of ecology which emphasized economic competition as the crucial ecological variable. Custom, race, religion, folkways, and techonology are considered as important factors in determining population patterns. See especially "Technology as a Factor in Ecological Succession." Parts appropriate for high school students.

307. Seeman, Albert L. "Communities in the Salt Lake Basin." *Economic Geography,* 14: 300–308, July 1938.

An ecological study of three Mormon communities, with an emphasis on culture and values as primary factors influencing community structure and development. Example of the socio-cultural approach to human ecology.

308. Sharp, Harry and Leo F. Schnore. "The Changing Color Composition of Metropolitan Areas." *Land Economics,* 58: 169–185, May 1962.

An analysis of population shifts in the twelve largest Standard Metropolitan Statistical Areas in the United States in 1960, with a detailed study of Detroit. Includes discussion of reasons for massive shifts and non-white movements to urban areas. Up-to-date material, raising some challenging questions.

309. *Shimkin, D. B. "The Economy of a Trapping Center: The Cast of Fort Yukon, Alaska." *Economic Development and Cultural Change,* 3: 219–240, April 1955.

The study of an Alaskan problem area dominated by a fur trapping economy. How economic, demographic, environmental, and organizational factors interact to produce an economic decline and social disorganization in the village. Useful as a case study; anthropological terminology may be eliminated.

310. Smith, P. J. "Calgary: A Study in Urban Pattern." *Economic Geography,* 38: 315–330, July 1962.

Discussion of the role of transportation in the development of land use patterns in a growing Canadian city, with an application of Homer Hoyt's sector theory. Useful as a case study to analyze urban growth models.

311. Steward, Julian H. *The Theory of Culture Change.* See No. 12,

312. Thompson, Laura. "The Relations of Men, Animals and Plants in an Island Community (Fiji)." George A. Theodorson, ed. *Studies in Human Ecology*. Evanston, Illinois: Row Peterson and Co., 1961, pp. 263–267.

A study of two "balanced" ecological systems on an island archipelago: one before human occupance, and one after.

313. *Turnbull, Colin M. "The Lesson of the Pygmies." *Scientific American*, 208: 28–37, January 1963. **SA–615**

How the Congo Pygmies of the Isuri rainforest adapt to the resources of their own and their neighbor's environments. This eminent anthropologist describes the informal social organization, the traditional values, and the technology of these forest people.

314. Washburn, Sherwood L. "Tools and Human Evolution." *Scientific American*, 203, September 1960. **SA–601**

Presents evidence that the use of tools predates man, so that technology is not an exclusively human attribute.

315. *White, Lynn. "The Historical Roots of Our Ecologic Crisis." *Science*, 155: 1203–1207, March 1967.

Analysis of the nature of environmental modification by man, advancing the view that human society will not be able to repair the ecological damage which modern science and technology has wrought until a spiritual revolution produces a new religion.

316. *Wulff, H. E. "The Qanats of Iran." *Scientific American*, 218: 94–107, April 1968. **S**

An admirable and lucid account of the means by which an arid plateau has been made partially habitable by the efforts of man in applying an ingenious water-conserving technology of subterranean conduits. Although it describes the case of Iran, this article greatly illuminates the case of the M'zab, in which similar means are used. Illustrated with materials suitable for the opaque projector.

317. *Wynne-Edwards, V. C. "Population Control in Animals." *Scientific American*, 208, August 1964. **SA–192**

Another key article, like Calhoun's (No. 280), which shows that there are social organizational controls (as well as death controls) on animal population by which equilibrium may be maintained through courtship, mating, and other control mechanisms.

IV. Visual Media in Ecological Study

Today there are an abundance of visual materials for enriching ecological study. Indeed, when they are not available ready-made, teachers can produce them using widely marketed kinds of duplicating apparatus. Maps, photographs, films, charts, graphs, and diagrams all can supplement regional case studies, helping students approach ecological factors and their interrelationships visually as well as verbally, making case study in the classroom vivid and meaningful.

In this chapter we suggest a number of visual aids for classroom use and describe how they enhance the study of ecosystems. We introduce techniques for their interpretation and construction, and finally demonstrate their use in a case study.

THE CONSTRUCTION AND INTERPRETATION
OF POPULATION MAPS

Maps are the primary visual tool of the geographer. They are of permanent importance in recording geographic data and depicting distributions of many types—population, rainfall, transportation, minerals, and racial or religious groups, to name a few. Thus they may be used to communicate collected research findings.

The distribution map is a primary aid to the student ecologist. As it depicts a single topic or theme, it is classified as a "topical" or "thematic" map. We will devote our discussion to one type, the population map—its nature, its construction, its interpretation, and finally, its use, along with other kinds of distribution maps, in discovering ecological relationships.

Before a class attempts to construct or interpret distribution maps, it is advisable to evaluate the students' familiarity with the fundamentals of mapping. If the teacher feels the necessity of reviewing or introducing general mapping concepts, such as projection, legends, scales, and symbols, there are many helpful guides available. One, Susan Marsh's *Teaching about Maps*,[1] is noted in the bibliography (No. 145).

A map that visually represents the spatial aspect of population may do it by depicting the absolute number of people living in a specific delimited region. Or it may show the ratio of the number of persons to a given unit of land area. We discuss both types of population map in this chapter.

The Representation of Absolute Values

In the construction of a map representing absolute values, the cartographer first collects census or other data available on the size of a particular population.[2] He then decides on some kind of representative geometric or pictorial symbol (such as dots or squares, stick men or bales of cotton).[3] The most frequently used, simplest symbol is the dot. Because of the relative ease of its construction and the visual impression of density it conveys, the dot map is one of the geographer's favorites, and this has led us to emphasize the uniform dot map of population for use in ecological studies. A simple uniform dot may may be seen in Figure 1.[4]

In a simple map depicting a small region, one dot may represent one person. A teacher might begin with this kind of population map in assigning his students the construction of a distribution map for their school. He asks them first to draw a bare map, outlining the school building plan, and then has them collect data on the number of children in each classroom. The students might decide to place one dot on the map for each student in the school. Perhaps some students will notice that the dots in many classrooms are so crowded that they are almost indistinguishable. This might lead them to decide that one dot should represent five students rather than one.[5] This type of exercise is helpful in demonstrating that each dot visually represents a specific number of units, in this case, children. The number of units assigned to each dot is commonly called the value of the dot. In this case, the value of the dot is five. There are many factors to be considered in the selection of dot values, and detailed discussions may be found in books on mapping listed in the bibliography.

Our student cartographers, in the meantime, are raising new questions about their map. Several students ask where in each classroom they should locate the dots. Should they arrange them uniformly in rows? Should they put them around the edges, or cluster them in the middle? In this particular case the junior map-makers know the exact location of each student, so they decide to place each dot according to the student seating arrangement.

Locating dots on a base map, in many instances, is much more difficult. The statistical data from which the cartographer works usually enumerates the population for fixed administrative units—counties, for instance, or blocks. With this information he can place his dots according to administrative divisions, but he does not know *where* in each

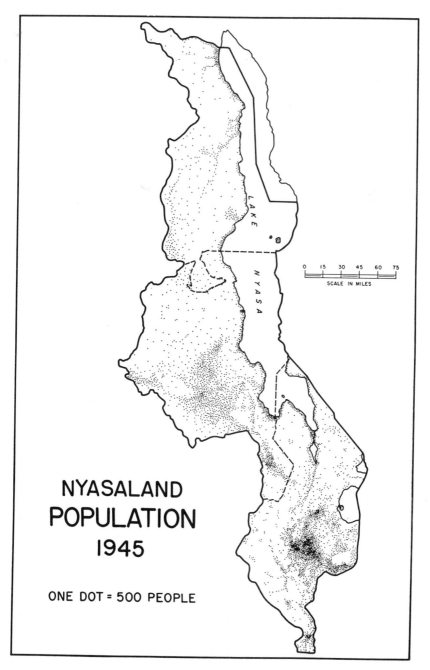

Figure 1. A simple uniform dot map.

division the population in reality resides. Instead of distributing the dots evenly, he may decide to place the dots in accordance with topography, transportation grids, or some other interpretive principle. In the Jos Plateau in Nigeria, for example, a field worker notes that a large portion of the population of a particular region resides in the hilly area, while the plains are relatively unoccupied, a principle of location also to be noted in Puerto Rico and in many other areas where either valley land is reserved for agriculture, or where defense considerations are paramount, or both. A carefully researched, well constructed map represents a clustering and scattering of population by the precise location of dots.[6]

A third consideration, after dot values and dot location, is selection of dot size. Size should depend first of all on the scale of the base map.[7] If the dots are too large, the region will appear to be too densely populated, and if they are too small, a faint, blurry effect will be produced. Mapping texts deal with this question to some extent. Of course, in the type of dot map we are concerned with, dots are of equal value and of uniform size.

The Representation of Relative Values

While the dot map described above depicts absolute values, the density map depicts relative values, such as the ratio of number of persons to a given unit of land area. If one thousand persons reside in an area of ten square miles, for example, the region has a population density ratio of one thousand divided by ten, or one hundred persons per square mile. The density map, although probably not used as frequently as the dot map, is still a primary tool in geography and demography.

Cartographers use several different kinds of map for representing relative values: the choropleth (Figure 2), the dasymetric (Figures 3 and 4), and the isopleth (Figure 5). We shall discuss all three mapping techniques here, concentrating on the choropleth method, however, because of its relative simplicity, ease of construction, and applicability to ecological study.

A good choropleth map shows at a glance the relative density of population for a particular region or nation. The choropleth map depicted in Figure 2, for example, shows density for civil divisions actually calculated from the statistics available for that region. Compare the use of areal symbols here and in Figure 1. Although the choropleth map is a relatively simple one to construct and interpret, there are a multitude of problems involved, of which both student and teacher should be aware. We shall indicate these problems by asking our junior cartographers,

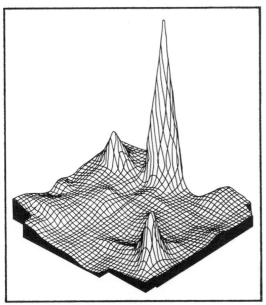

Figure 2. The smoothed statistical surface (above) is a model which represents continuous population density variation in an urbanized area. The choropleth map (below) is a rendering of the same area by the choropleth mapping techniques described in the text. Note that in passing from one level of abstraction to another, some information is lost, but the pattern remains clearly identifiable.

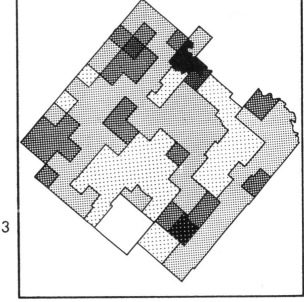

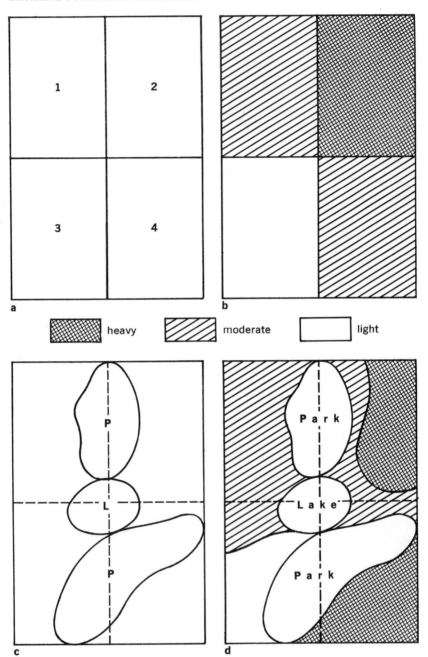

Figure 3. A simplified representation of stages in dasymetric mapping. See the discussion on page 110.

now experts in dot mapping, to construct a choropleth map for their school district, showing population density.

The first task, as in all mapping exercises, is to choose a base map whose scale is appropriate to the task at hand. Since the school district under consideration is relatively small in area, the students can construct a rather large-scale map on a piece of paper about the size of an open textbook.

From their experience with dot maps, the students know that next they must collect the data that they will symbolically represent on their map. However, when they consult the census, they find a listing of statistics for the three large counties, but also for the eleven parishes comprising the same district. The class is confronted with the problem of choosing between two methods of enumeration. Should they choose the smaller or the larger civil divisions?

Some students remember from their dot map construction that data for regions *per se* does not represent variations in density, and may see that the larger the census division employed, the greater the potential overgeneralization. Since the use of the three counties does not account sufficiently for variations within the district, and since the students do not have time for field work and map consultation, they wisely choose to employ the parish data.

We should note parenthetically that when population data can be obtained only for large political units, the cartographer often uses a supplementary technique, known as dasymetric mapping. Dasymetric mapping is a technique which attempts to eliminate the arbitrary effect of census or political boundaries on mapping by correcting the mapped distributions with the help of other data.[8] Suppose regions 1, 2, 3, 4 in A of Figure 3 are census districts, and suppose that the population densities can be represented as they are in B. By consulting another map (in C) we find a lake and two parks. We remap, adjusting boundaries and zones as in D. Note that region 4 (shown by the dotted lines), which was only moderately dense formerly, now is shown as dense because the effective residential area is smaller.

Data used in the correction of the overgeneralized choropleth map is frequently found in aerial photos and field reports as well as in other kinds of maps. In such a way, variables like cultivatable land can be taken into account. The effect, on a larger scale, is shown in Figure 4.[9] Since a number of calculations are required, however, we do not recommend this technique for student use.[10]

After the students have decided which political regions to use, they must determine the population density within each region. This is done by dividing the number of persons living in the region by the number

109

of square miles (or, outside the U. S., square kilometers) contained in the region. As many sources of population statistics do not provide information about land area, the following method may be used to approximate it. The students overlay a map of the region in question with a sheet of graph paper and count the approximate number of boxes covering the region. Then they determine the area represented by 1 square by using the scale usually provided at the bottom of the map. If the length of 5 boxes corresponds to 10 miles, for instance, then the length of 1 box represents 2 miles and the area covered by 1 box represents 4 square miles. A region on the map covered by 10 boxes would have an area of approximately 40 square miles. If the population of the region is 4400, the density then would be 110 (per square mile).

The students then decide to represent densities ranging from 0–25 by one symbol, those from 25–50 by another, those from 50–100 by another, and so forth. This process of choosing the limits of class intervals is a difficult one,[11] but, if necessary, limits can be assigned by the teacher utilizing the judgment of the group. Engaging students in such a process is important, because it familiarizes them with the great degree of subjectivity involved in map-making. They soon see that maps take on very different appearances, depending on the limits chosen for each class interval. How then, should the class depict the chosen density intervals on their map?

One student suggests using three different designs, x's, dots, and parallel lines. At a glance, one can not tell the most dense from the least dense without carefully checking the key. A more effective system, which would depict areas of dense and sparse population at a glance, is suggested. Why not show increasing density by grading intervals from white to black, or from light color to dark color? This way we can immediately tell the densest areas by their dark tint, and the sparsely populated areas by their light tint. One student even suggests having original designs but grading them also, making the x's very thin, the parallel lines extremely thick and dark, and the dots intermediate. (Note the use of a similar technique in Figure 2.) Different designs are used for each interval, but shading from light to dark gives the impression of increasing density.[12]

There are many problems involved in choropleth shading, as there are in all other aspects of map construction. Before interpreting population maps in the classroom, both teacher and student should be aware of the difficulties in construction. In both dot and choropleth maps, poor construction can be misleading. We do not want distorted distributions caused by poor construction to be accepted by our students as "facts." Thus, in interpreting dot maps, students should be aware of the effects

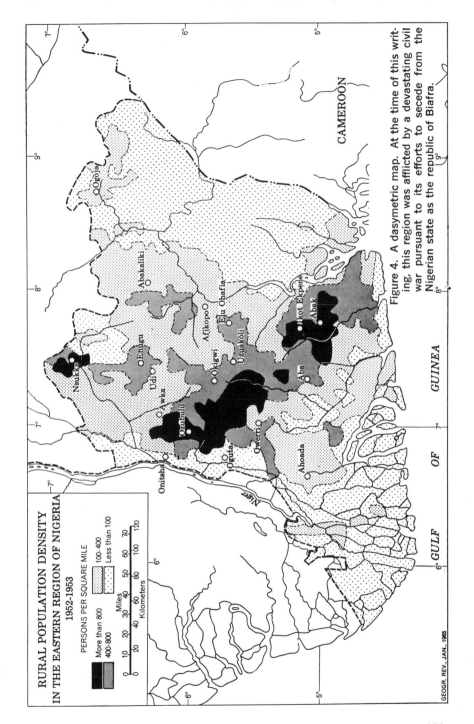

RURAL POPULATION DENSITY
IN THE EASTERN REGION OF NIGERIA
1952-1953

PERSONS PER SQUARE MILE

More than 800
400-800
100-400
Less than 100

Miles
0 10 20 30 40 50 60 70
0 20 40 60 80 100 120
Kilometers

Figure 4. A dasymetric map. At the time of this writing, this region was afflicted by a devastating civil war pursuant to its efforts to secede from the Nigerian state as the republic of Biafra.

GEOGR. REV., JAN., 1965

111

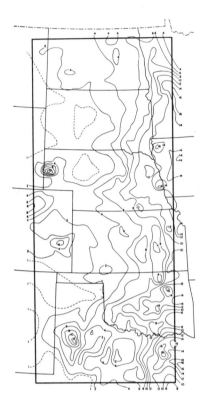

Figure 5. An isopleth map showing population density.

of assigning dot value, placement, and size. Similarly, in choropleth mapping, they should be cognizant of the effects of unit size, scale of interval, and shading method. A critical analysis of the construction of ready-made maps, prior to interpretation, is always useful. Teachers should seriously consider the problems noted above when selecting maps for student use.

Another method of revealing density patterns, which we note only briefly here, is isopleth mapping. It is probably among the most difficult of all types of population map to construct and interpret. Rather than depicting population density by areal symbols, this method involves the drawing of lines through areas of the same population density class,[13] as depicted in Figure 5. Lines rather than areas are given a value. Since isopleth maps are difficult to construct and interpret, they are considered by the authors to be of limited value as visual tools in secondary school ecological study, and no effort is made here to analyze their qualities in detail.[14]

Cautions on the Use of Density Maps

The density map is an excellent tool, but an often misused one. It may be a visual starting point for analysis, but one must apply knowledge of other ecological factors in order to comprehend the true meaning of density for that region. Students should not infer "facts" about economic well-being from population density alone, for it is only through an understanding of the dynamic interrelationship of all the ecological factors that we can understand the nature of a region.[15]

In fact, it is problem a good exercise for students to compile lists of high and low density areas in the world and organize the areas of the world into high and low level-of-living categories. Finding out why high population density is coupled with high levels of living in some parts of the world and with low levels of living in others is an outgrowth of this kind of exercise. A typological structure is shown in Figure 6. (The Norton Ginsburg atlas contains all of the data requisite for this exercise.) This is a useful way to lead the students to look for the ecological factors, other than population density, associated with economic well-being. This is a technique adaptable for showing the relation between any two ecological factors.

Scale

A vital factor to be considered when constructing and interpreting population maps of all types is the concept of *scale*. Maps are constructed proportional to the earth's surface, and the larger the scale, the closer the map is to reality. An exact representation of the earth's surface would have to be as large as the earth itself, or that portion of the earth under consideration. (Even when one inch on the map represents one mile on the earth's surface, a scale of 1:63,360,[16] this would require an unwieldy mass of paper.) Most maps, especially those in textbooks and atlases, are much smaller in scale, usually ranging in scale from 1:10,000,000 to 1:20,000,000.

When selecting maps for classroom use, teachers should be aware that small-scale maps are greatly reduced in size and are usually limited in detail. A single-page textbook-size map of world population distribution, for example, would not be a very appropriate tool for the study of the population distribution of Nigeria. Teachers will be equipped, after some experience, to determine the map scale appropriate for their particular use. They will usually find large-scale maps preferable in most ecological study.

The Representation of Change

We must present a caution to teachers who intend to use distribution maps as tools in ecological studies. The maps we have already discussed,

LIVING LEVEL

DENSITY		High	Medium	Low
	High	A E F	N P S	B G X
	Medium	C L U	D J Z	H Y
	Low	I K	M R V W	O Q T

In this sample, no consistent relationship between
density and living level is demonstrated.

LIVING LEVEL

DENSITY		High	Medium	Low
	High	A H R E K T G L Y	none	none
	Medium	none	C M D S I W J X	none
	Low	none	none	B O U F P V N Q F

In this sample, there is a perfect relationship between density and living level;
high living level is always associated with high density, and so forth.

Figure 6. Classifying Countries A–Z by Two Measures

114

both those that show absolute values (dot maps) and those that show ratios (density maps) are static. They depict a distribution at a single point in time. However, distributions themselves are not static, nor are the associations between various factors that may be distributed—population, environmental, organizational, technological, socio-psychological variables. The distinguished American geographer, Clyde Kohn, calls this the phenomenon of *fluidity*.[17]

Observing distributions over time adds a new dimension to the visual technique of analyzing ecological relationships. Maps depicting distributions at different points in time may be compared to help students visualize change in a ecosystem. Or maps of rates of change themselves may be constructed, showing the percent of increase or decrease of population or other ecological factors over time.

The teacher and class may find it worthwhile, where data exist (as in the United Nations Demographic and Statistical Yearbook), to select a region and map population growth, industrial growth, change in per capita energy consumption,[18] or the change in some other variable. Population change, for instance, may be calculated by figuring the percentage of increase or decrease in population occurring between two censuses in the various subdivisions of the region.[19] (The necessary background in the fundamental concepts and definitions of population dynamics is available in the volume by Hertzberg cited in the annotated bibliography.)[20] After calculating and mapping the percentage of growth for each subdivision of a region, a pattern of change emerges, and some subdivisions may be said to have "above average" growth, others "average " growth, and still others "less than average" growth or even a decline (see Figure 7).

This leads directly into a consideration of all the other ecological factors and their interrelationships. What other factors are related to this particular pattern? Why are there changes in some areas and not in others? And what is the significance of the change for the ecosystem as a whole? Students might apply data previously collected in an effort to answer these questions, or be led to collect new data. Then through the construction of rate maps for other factors, such as technological change, and through the comparison of maps, some answers might be discovered. Techniques for comparing maps are discussed further on, in the development of the Rockland County case, and again on pages 128–130.

The Transition Map

Although there is no absolute relationship between density *per se* and level of living, a process of *demographic transition* has been observed, in

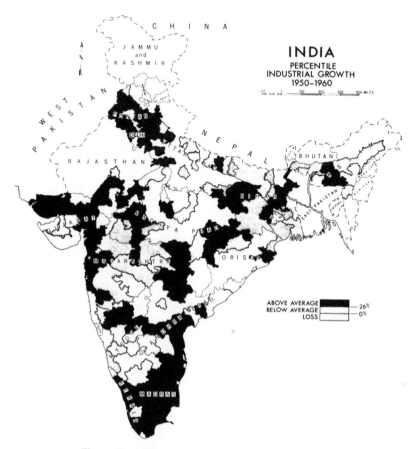

Figure 7. A rate map, showing industrial growth.

which a region or nation passes through a series of stages ending in a final period of low birth and death rates with slow population growth. The process has been described as a three-stage experience,[21] the first stage demonstrating high birth and death rates and a slow growth rate, the second (or "explosion") stage demonstrating continuing high birth rates and rapidly declining death rates, resulting in accelerated population growth, and the third stage demonstrating a low death rate now balanced by a low birth rate, resulting once again in the slow growth.

Chung has mapped the demographic transition for the twentieth century on a world scale, and has suggested that the timing and duration of the transition varies from region to region.[22] A series of maps showing how the process may be graphically represented are given, with an explanation, in Figure 8.

116

With the crude birth and death rate data provided by the *United Nations Demographic Yearbook* or other national and regional sources, a class may construct transition maps similar to those presented by Chung for a region of interest, possibly their own.* They may then analyze the timing and duration of the transition in their region, and attempt to relate these phenomena to other ecological factors. Chung suggests, for example, that size of population, technological innovations of death control, and perceptions concerning family size all relate to the timing of the "population explosion" of the "Third World." Certainly the technology, social organization, environment, social psychology, and population are variables that should all be considered by the students.

* As noted by Hertzberg, Chung, and others, reliability of data varies from region to region and from source to source. In any study of population, ecological and otherwise, teachers should be aware of limitations and distortions in the data, and should convey to their students the necessity of evaluating the reliability of all data.

Figures 8a–c. Stages of demographic transition for the world (pp. 118–120). The three stages of demographic transition are distinguished in all three maps by the following key.

    Stage One (high birth and death rates, and a slow growth rate)

    Stage Two (continuing high birth rates and rapidly declining death rates, with accelerated population growth)

    Stage Two—Alternate (moderate birth and death rates, and a resultant slow rate of growth)

    Stage Three (low birth and death rates, and a slow growth rate)

    Figure 8c shows that in 1960 most of the underdeveloped nations either were still in Stage One or were in the explosive Stage Two, while nations in most of North America, Europe, and parts of Oceania as well as the Soviet Union and Japan had reached Stage Three. Chung suggests that the various nations enter the stages at different times and remain in them for varying lengths of time—thus, that the timing and duration of the transition varies from region to region.

Stage One   Stage Two   Stage Two—   Stage Three
                              Alternate

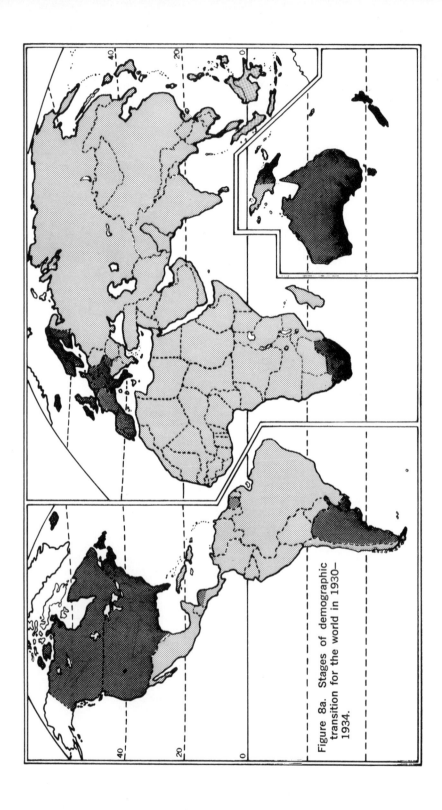

Figure 8a. Stages of demographic transition for the world in 1930—1934.

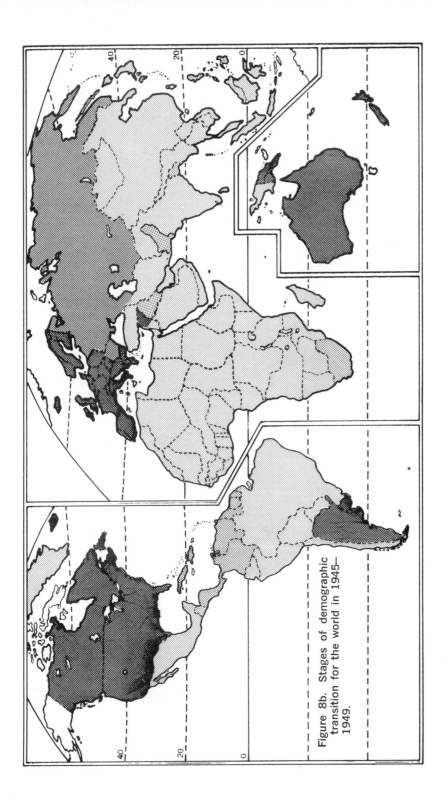

Figure 8b. Stages of demographic transition for the world in 1945–1949.

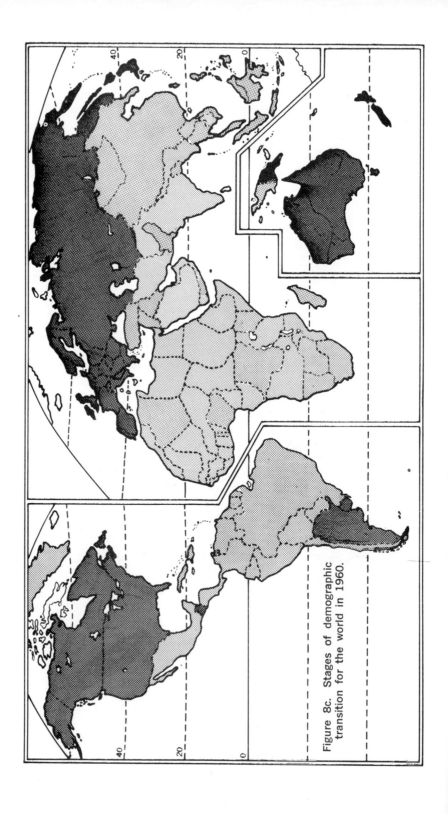

Figure 8c. Stages of demographic transition for the world in 1960.

A DEMONSTRATION CASE STUDY:
ROCKLAND COUNTY, NEW YORK

In order to demonstrate the utility of maps as tools for ecological study in the classroom, we have prepared a study of Rockland County, New York in which we make use of a number of the techniques discussed in the preceding pages. These notes on demographic changes in a New York suburb are not at all intended to be exhaustive, but are rather intended to point the way in which lessons may be developed to combine mapping, simple graph work, and regional observations in an ecological framework, analyzing and interpreting the direction of local demographic change.

The Use of Areal Association

The technique known as areal association or correlation will be used in developing the Rockland County case. It involves the simultaneous inspection of two or more phenomena over a particular region to discover possible relationships. For example, several maps of a single region, each depicting a particular distribution, are presented for student analysis. Using distribution maps, the class may visually examine, for example, distribution patterns of rainfall, minerals, crops, transportation facilities, as well as population. Norton Ginsburg has constructed a series of choropleth maps on a world scale which facilitate this type of comparison and analysis.

In order to facilitate comparability, the maps should have a common base and scale, as the Ginsburg maps do. There are several methods available to the classroom teacher for simultaneous presentation of two or more distribution maps. A number of these will be discussed at the end of this chapter. One of the best is the use of transparent overlays with the opaque projector.

While inspecting two or more maps, students will note that in some cases two or more distributions occur together. A geographer would say that these phenomena *covary*. For example, observation of topographic, transportation, and population maps of a hypothetical region might lead students to note that populations cluster in the hilly areas and along rail transportation routes, but not along waterways. The discovery of covariance in the first two instances might encourage further examination of ecological relationships among these factors.

Teachers and their classes should be cautioned that the covariance of two factors does not prove either causality or necessity. It merely suggests a possible relationship, for another unknown factor or factors might have contributed to the mutual occurrence, or it may merely be a result of coincidence.

121

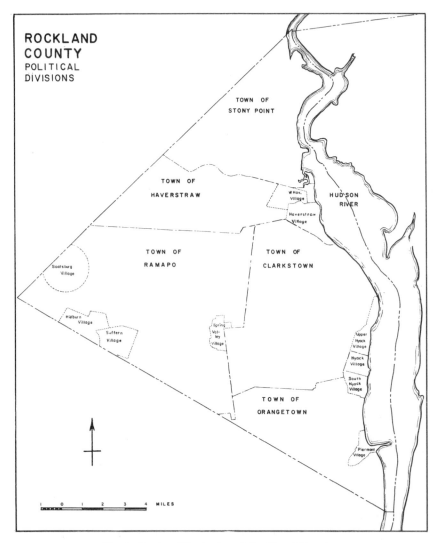

ROCKLAND
COUNTY
POLITICAL
DIVISIONS

TOWN OF
STONY POINT

TOWN OF
HAVERSTRAW

W Hav.
Village

HUDSON
RIVER

Haverstraw
Village

Sloatsburg
Village

TOWN OF
RAMAPO

TOWN OF
CLARKSTOWN

Hilburn
Village

Suffern
Village

Spring
Val-
ley
Village

Upper
Nyack
Village

Nyack
Village

South
Nyack
Village

TOWN OF
ORANGETOWN

Piermont
Village

0   1   2   3   4   MILES

Figure 9. A political map of Rockland County.

Several nineteenth- and early twentieth-century geographers argued, for example, that population clusters in river valleys or fertile areas were *caused* by the favorable environment of these regions. They did not explain, however, why similar regions remained relatively unoccupied, or why unfavorable desert or mountainous regions in many instances supported extremely dense populations. We noted previously the need to be very careful with deterministic views and causal explanations in

122

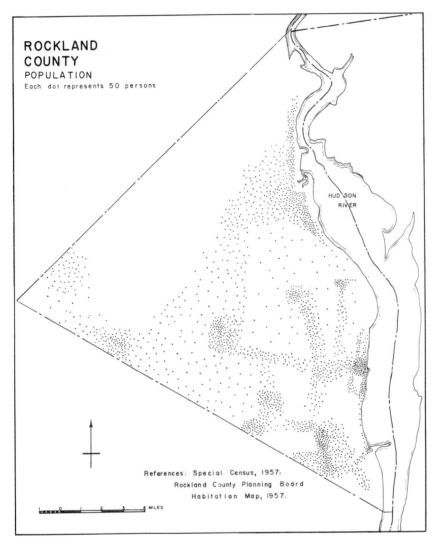

Figure 10. Population in Rockland County.

ecological study. It is more important to examine how the organization, technology, and social psychology of the ecosystem mediate between the population and its environment. Although areal association is a valuable, stimulating technique, the spatial correlation of phenomena must be supplemented by considering the role of other ecological factors, not only those depicted on the distribution maps.

123

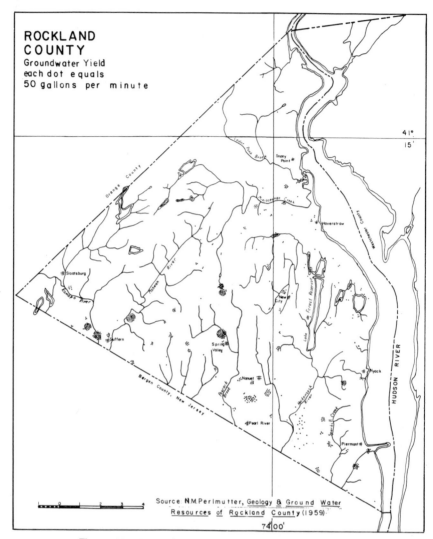

Figure 11. Groundwater resources in Rockland County.

Population Change in Rockland County, New York

Within a commuting radius of New York City lies the suburban region comprising Rockland County. A glance at the maps in Figures 9, 10, and 11 will show that the area is organized politically into five towns and a number of villages, but that the population is unequally distributed over the county and, indeed, that large portions of the towns of Ramapo, Haverstraw, and Stony Point are empty. On the other hand,

124

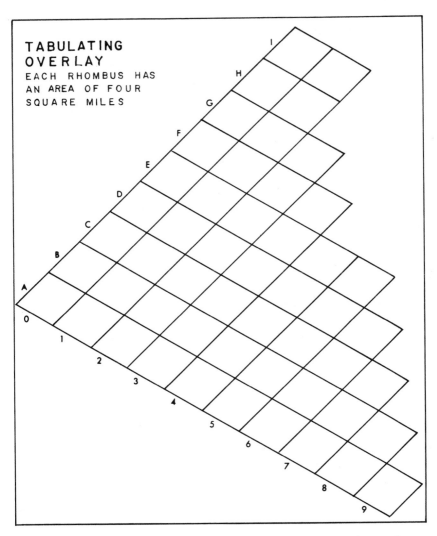

TABULATING
OVERLAY
EACH RHOMBUS HAS
AN AREA OF FOUR
SQUARE MILES

Figure 12. A tabulating overlay for the comparison of Rockland County data.

bands of dense settlement seem to run from east to west along a Nyack-Spring Valley axis, and from south to north along a line from Orange-town almost to Haverstraw Village. The water resource map tells us that both groundwater and surface water are used as water supplies for the region, and that there may be a relationship between hydrology and demography in the area.

The drainage pattern is produced by a line of cliffs which start to the west of Haverstraw (south of Minisceongo Creek) and curve around

125

to the southeast, following the line of the Hudson River. These cliffs are called the Palisades, and most of the drainage flows inland from them into the watershed and valley of the Hackensack River. Another highland area, the Ramapo hills, lies along the northwestern boundary of the county and serves to separate the Ramapo, Mahwah, and Cedar Pond watersheds from the remainder of the county. Between the Ramapo hills and the Palisades lies an undulating valley developed on a base of porous red sandstone, which is an excellent aquifer.

To what extent is the demographic pattern of the region related to the range of ecological dimensions? Let us start by examining the relationship of demography to the environment. The valley land is occupied; the hill land is not. While the crest of the Palisades is largely left unoccupied, there are population clusters along the narrow Hudson River littoral, such as the Nyacks, where (along the line of a small creek) there is a gap, giving access to the western portion of the county. Roads have been developed leading toward Spring Valley and Suffern along this route. Another gap in the Palisades, in the vicinity of Piermont, is likewise densely populated.

Passes and river valleys have an obvious importance in the settlement pattern—what of groundwater? The labelled grid shown in Figure 12, when overlaid on the maps of population and groundwater, enables one to tabulate the groundwater yield as it compares with the population in each grid cell. Five cells of abnormally heavy groundwater use appear, corresponding to sites where industry has begun to concentrate, in Hillburn, Pearl River, Sloatsburg, and Spring Valley. This represents a new trend in groundwater use—industrial rather than merely residential—and suggests the pressure that may ultimately be placed on the water supplies available to Rockland County.

Having explored the relationship of terrain and hydrology to population distribution, we may comment briefly on the relationship of social organization. Much of the empty space on the population map which corresponds to highland area has been set aside as park, recreational, and watershed land by government action and private bequest. Population clusters on the Hudson River are older than those a little further inland because of the transportation flows that characterized the river in the age of water transportation, linking the metropolis of New York City with Hudson Valley towns, in particular with Haverstraw, a producer of brick from which much of New York City was constructed, and Nyack, a busy river port of supply for agricultural products.

With the development of the technology of the automobile and the high-speed motor road, the interior areas of the county have been opened up to dense settlement, and ultimately (as in the five areas of heavy water use noted above) to industry as well. The technology of trucking and electrical energy distribution has facilitated the dissemination throughout the county of firms whose production processes depend on extensive one-story factories with lengthy assembly lines built on large areas of flat land, oriented to the New York metropolitan market.*

These changes in demography, environment, technology, and social organization have been accompanied, in turn, by a change in psychological perspective on the part of the dwellers in the county. No longer oriented to agricultural activity and the bustling river towns, the population is increasingly oriented to the metropolis via the motor road and rubber-tire transportation. Thus Nyack and Haverstraw are experiencing relative economic decline, while Spring Valley (the principle interior node on the highway network) and the roadsides of the major arteries are experiencing rapid growth, shifting the demographic center of gravity westward. The overall ecological changes make it possible for denser populations to be sustained at a higher material level of living, but economic pressures are brought upon parks and vacant land.

READY-MADE VISUAL MATERIALS

A number of excellent books and articles deal with the advantages of supplementing the curriculum with visual materials.[23] It is not our purpose here to enumerate the many cogent arguments for the use of such materials in the classroom. Instead, we attempt to demonstrate the usefulness of visual media for classroom ecological study, for, if used judiciously, pictures, aerial photographs, films, filmstrips, slides, and transparencies can play a vital role in the study of ecological phenomena and their interrelationships.

Such material is not intended as a substitute for the collection of data by students, but only as a supplement. Many phenomena, particularly those occurring in foreign lands, may be difficult for students to visualize, and in most cases students cannot venture out into the field. However, through graphics, we can bring the field to them. For almost every regional case study, the teacher and his students can collect a variety of visual materials that will help in understanding various physical and cultural components of the region.

Visual aids may be used to portray a particular aspect of an ecological factor in a region. For example, a picture of the Mozabite method of drawing groundwater conveys visually an aspect of technology quite

* Relevant maps are available from the Hagstrom Map Company or from the Rockland County Planning Board.

difficult to comprehend through verbal description alone. Similarly, a photo of the landscape and nature features of the Iraqui marshes will reveal a good deal about the marsh environment of that region. Visual aids often reveal relationships. What might a picture of the Saharan limestone plateaus dotted with irrigation ditches and *wadi* gardens say about the ecology of the M'zab? And they may demonstrate change as well. Pictures of the same region, taken over a period of time, can be analyzed by students to uncover changing relationships.

Visual media may be used throughout all phases of a particular regional study. Pictures, films, filmstrips, or slides, for example, can be used for introductory purposes, as motivating devices, or as aids to familiarize students with aspects of a society. They may be integrated into class discussion to highlight a particular aspect of technology or to reinforce the importance of a particular relationship. They may be used to summarize or review characteristics of a regional ecosystem.

However, visual aids are not only sources of information. They also stimulate thinking and encourage students to draw inferences, exercise analytical skills, and raise pertinent questions. Visual materials, unfortunately, may also be misused in the classroom. It is up to the teacher carefully to select and preview those materials that he feels will enhance students' understanding of ecological phenomena.

In this section we make a short survey of the various ready-made visual materials that may be most useful to the teacher presenting regional case studies and discuss some of the sources of each.

Maps

The relevance of map construction and interpretation is discussed in the preceding portions of this chapter. Professionally made maps are available from a variety of sources: map companies, textbooks, regional monographs, journal and magazine articles, atlases, and national and international agencies.[24] All these provide a variety of physical, political, and thematic maps.

A particularly useful tool is the political and/or physical outline of a nation, region, or subregion. Outline maps are available in forms appropriate both for large-group and for individual use. Large wall-size slate outline maps may be marked by students with chalk to note various distributions and activities. Also available are large wall outline maps lithographed on heavy white paper. These maps are frequently supplemented by transparent overlays, on which students may draw and easily erase so that the maps can be used over and over again. In some cases, outline maps are printed in the form of transparencies which may be projected onto a screen and viewed by the entire class. A tool quite useful for the individual student is the desk outline map, enabling him to construct his own map of the region under consideration.

A recent mapping innovation which is particularly useful in exploring the environmental dimension of the ecosystem is the vinyl relief map, a three-dimensional representation of the earth's surface that enables students through touch and observation to visualize the land form of a region. Such relief maps are available for various world nations and for several states and United States Geological Survey quadrangles.[25]

Flat Pictures

Photographs of all sorts are applicable in every stage of ecological analysis. At the same time, they are probably the most abundant, inexpensive, and readily available visual resource. If it is difficult to procure films, filmstrips, or slides for a particular region, in most cases it is possible to acquire at least a few pertinent pictures. Good sources are journal and magazine articles, books, textbooks, and newspapers. Stills from many commercial, industrial, and educational films may be acquired inexpensively upon request. Several guides to sources for this type of material are noted in the bibliography.

The aerial photograph, or photograph of the earth's surface taken from the air, is in a special category. It is a rich visual source and has in many cases been overlooked by secondary school teachers. The size and nature of the area photographed depends on a number of different factors. In some cases the photo includes only natural phenomena such as vegetation, land form, and soils. In other cases, the photo depicts cultural phenomena such as housing, land use, transportation routes, and general human activity. An aerial photograph, properly interpreted, will tell a student exactly where a population lives. Such information is not revealed by census statistics. Furthermore, it is an *actual* rather than symbolic representation of a region.

There are two types of aerial photograph. The vertical photo, which more closely resembles a map, is taken from the air with the camera pointed vertically downward. The oblique photo is taken with the camera pointed downward at an angle. While the oblique photograph shows a more familiar picture, the vertical picture is the more valuable tool because it provides a more detailed, less obstructed view and does not distort the perspective.[26]

The vertical photograph may also be studied stereoptically. When one views a photograph, the effect is that of an object seen with one eye, and the depth illusion is lost. Certain objects therefore may be unrecognizable in photographs. If aerial photographs are presented in stereo pairs, the depth illusion is retained. A stereo pair is produced by photographing a region from two different points and then superimposing the images through the use of a stereoscopic viewer.[27] Stereo pairs for aerial photographs of some regions of the world and inexpensive plastic stereoscopes are available from commercial companies[28] and from various national governmental agencies. Accurate measurements of heights may be made by photogrammetric means on stereo pairs.

Aerial photography is one of the best available methods for depicting ecological change. Two sets of photographs, taken twenty years apart, will reveal quite different natural and cultural features and patterns. Students may apply their knowledge of the ecological phenomena of the region in order to interpret the differences portrayed in the two aerial photographs. Analyses of this kind might lead to further questioning and investigation as well.

Aerial photographs present special problems of interpretation, but it is certainly worthwhile for both student and teacher to become acquainted with the relevant methods and techniques. Several volumes on this topic, such as the Susan Marsh series, are listed in the bibliography. Sources of aerial photographs are also noted in the bibliography. While many are expensive to purchase, monographs and magazine and journal articles in particular are rich and inexpensive sources.* With the methods of presentation noted in the next section of this chapter, teachers may present such aerial photos to the entire class.

Other Visual Aids

Certain visual aids are produced specifically for projection. Slides, filmstrips, and motion pictures are the primary sources in this category. Although these materials are often difficult to obtain and usually more expensive than those previously mentioned, they too play an important role in ecological study.

Relevant slides, filmstrips, and motion pictures are available for

---

* An especially good inexpensive source of aerial photographs that is easily available to the teacher is the Geological Survey of the U. S. Department of the Interior. For many parts of the U. S., 9″ by 9″ prints of 12-square-mile areas are available at $1.00 each (lower prices on multiple orders). Photo indexes may be secured for the area in which the teacher is interested, from which the particular photographs desired may be selected. At additional cost, the 9″ by 9″ plates may be enlarged to one square yard, suitable for wall display. Individual houses, artifacts, and elements of land use are easily visible on these prints. A series of prints may be purchased showing the transformation of the same 12-square-mile area in time as the ecological system changes. In particular, this is useful in connection with the Morrisville case study. A brochure entitled *Aerial Photographic Reproductions* is available free from Map Information Office, U. S. Geological Survey, Washington, D. C. 20242.

practically every nation in the world. The many excellent films dealing with limited regions and communities in particular are ideal for ecological study and in many cases are the most stimulating of all visual tools, for they depict a society in action and may reveal process and change more readily than other visual materials. They are extensively noted, with guides to their sources, in the bibliography. Teachers should note that in some cases films and filmstrips may be borrowed free, and that many may be rented at a minimal cost. Local university and other libraries frequently loan or rent films and filmstrips.

We have suggested a few types of visual materials thought to be most applicable to ecological study. As in any discipline, visual materials must be used purposefully, selectively, and sparingly. We have not time here to cover the many techniques for selecting, evaluating, and interpreting visual materials. We hope that we have helped to orient the teacher toward the type of material that will enrich ecological study.

CLASS- AND TEACHER-PRODUCED MATERIALS

In many instances where it is difficult for teachers to acquire ready-made maps, pictures, slides, films, or filmstrips for a particular study, the teacher and class might want to create their own visual materials. A primary activity, already described, is student map construction. The material requirements are few. Usually only collected data, paper, and pencils are needed. Students simultaneously become familiar with the ecological data for their region and acquaint themselves with the problems involved in map construction and interpretation.

Illustrating particular aspects of the ecology of a region is a valuable exercise—for example, drawing a picture of the process by which the Mozabites utilize groundwater. Crude schematic drawings are sufficient to represent material in a clear and comprehensive manner.

The teacher's and students' own photographs may be a valuable resource. If the class is doing a study of their own community ecosystem, they may take pictures of relevant ecological phenomena and inter-relationships on camera field trips. Or the teacher may bring in pictures of ecological features of various regions taken during his travels. 35-mm camera slides are specially valuable, for then the photographs may be projected and simultaneously interpreted by the class members.

A simple technique for using pictures or artifacts from the society under discussion is to pass them around the classroom. This procedure should be used when no other method is available, for it has several disadvantages. Students cannot simultaneously view the material and have a tendency to lose interest after having inspected the material and passed it on. A classroom activity that helps to eliminate this problem is called "the whip." As the material is passed around the room, each student is asked to make a comment about some feature or to point out a relationship implied by it.

The opaque projector is a most valuable tool for displaying all kinds of visual material.[29] It "shoots" an image, enlarges it, and throws it on a screen or wall, so that it may be seen by the entire class at one time. It has a built-in disadvantage in that it ordinarily must be used in a darkened classroom. Pictures, student-constructed maps, aerial photographs, statistical data, and even artifacts may be shown.

Another more recent and often more useful tool is the overhead projector. This piece of equipment is smaller and less difficult to handle than the opaque projector. It is not necessary to use it in a darkened classroom. It is also constructed in such a manner that the teacher may face the class and lead discussion while the image is being viewed. The overhead projector is constructed particularly for use with transparencies, which are translucent sheets usually made of clear plastic, acetate, or a similar material. Any type of writing or drawing may be added in grease pencil or translucent inks and removed, when desired, with a piece of dry cotton.[30] Ready-made transparencies, such as outline maps and population and other distribution maps are available from several map and other commercial companies.[31] Teachers may also obtain unmarked clear plastic sheets on which students may draw their own maps and other images, projecting their finished product onto the screen and allowing the entire class to comment on their work.

We noted previously that when students inspect maps for areal association and covariance, they should observe several distributions simultaneously. One excellent method of doing this is through the use of transparent overlays. A series of distribution maps for the same region may be drawn on transparencies and may be placed one over the other. The class, for example, may have prepared distribution maps of population, topography, transportation, and agricultural land use for the Jos Plateau region. First the population map is projected on the screen for student analysis. Any other of the separate maps, of course, may be selected to be shown first. The students then may choose to superimpose any other map on the first, simultaneously showing two distributions, which may be examined for areal association. In this manner, any number of distributions from two to eight may be overlaid, compared, and analyzed. This technique is difficult to surpass. However, when proper equipment is not available, the class may draw several distributions on the same sheet of paper, a method frequently used by professional cartographers. The patterns of distribution are, of course, less clear, the map in many cases becomes cluttered, and certain distributions may not be easily removed. Two American geographers[32] have suggested superimposing a set of successive slide patterns over a base map on a chalkboard. As each slide is projected, its pattern is recorded by means of chalk outlines, resulting in a number of distributions appearing on a single base map. This is a useful technique, but it produces general outlines rather than specific patterns. Also, it does not have the flexibility of the transparent overlay method and also requires the preparation of slides, in itself a difficulty.

Where visual materials are available in forms inappropriate for classroom study and an opaque projector is not available or not practical, transparencies and slides may be made by the teacher. Any picture, statistical table, or aerial photograph may be transferred to a transparency using a Thermofax machine.[33] Placing the material under a sheet of special foil and running it through produces an exact transparent copy within seconds. The results are very similar in photocopying, but a 35-mm slide is produced. The material is photographed with a 35-mm single-lens reflex camera either in sunlight outdoors or on a simple copying stand indoors with proper lighting. The resulting slide may then be projected.[34]

In Conclusion

We have tried to discuss the most useful methods for supplementing classroom ecological study with visual materials. We realize that the availability of materials varies from school to school; thus we have included a variety of methods, with equipment and materials ranging from the simplest to the most sophisticated.

NOTES

[1] Susan Marsh, *Teaching About Maps*. Darien, Connecticut: Teachers Publishing Corporation, 1965.
[2] See "Statistical Sources," beginning on page 61 in the annotated bibliography, for sample sources.
[3] Jan O. M. Broek, *Geography, Its Scope and Spirit*. Columbus, Ohio: Charles E. Merrill, 1965, p. 66.
[4] The following are particularly useful in discussing map symbolizations in greater detail: Jan O. M. Broek, *Geography, Its Scope and Spirit* (Columbus, Ohio: Charles E. Merrill, 1965); F. J. Monkhouse and H. R. Wilkinson, *Maps and Diagrams* (London: Methuen, 1952); Arthur H. Robinson, *Elements of Cartography*, 2nd ed. (New York: John Wiley and Sons, 1960).
[5] Zoe A. Thralls, *The Teaching of Geography*. New York: Appleton-Century-Crofts, 1958, p. 41.
[6] Broek, *op. cit.*, p. 67.
[7] Monkhouse and Wilkinson, *op. cit.*, p. 22.

[8] Wilbur Zelinsky, *A Prologue to Population Geography.* Englewood Cliffs, New Jersey: Prentice-Hall, 1966, p. 9.

[9] *Ibid.*

[10] For a discussion of dasymetric map construction see Robinson, *op. cit.,* pp. 174–175 and 145.

[11] See J. Ross MacKay, "An Analysis of Isopleth and Choropleth Intervals," *Economic Geography,* 31:71–81, January 1955.

[12] Discussed in Monkhouse and Wilkinson, *op. cit.,* pp. 34–39.

[13] Broek, *op. cit.,* pp. 68–69.

[14] For details see: J. Ross Mackay, "Some Problems and Techniques in Isopleth Mapping," *Economic Geography,* 27:1–9, January 1951; Robinson, *op. cit.,* Chapter 10, "Mapping Three-Dimensional Data," pp. 178–194.

[15] Henry S. Hunker, *Erich W. Zimmermann's Introduction to World Resources.* New York: Harper and Row, 1964, p. 138.

[16] Broek, *op. cit.,* p. 66.

[17] Clyde Kohn, "Basic Concepts of Geography and Their Development in the Classroom," *in* Edwin Fenton, *Teaching the New Social Studies in Secondary Schools.* New York: Holt, Rinehart and Winston, 1966, p. 410.

[18] Norton Ginsburg, *Atlas of Economic Development.* Chicago: University of Chicago Press, 1961, p. 87.

[19] Monkhouse and Wilkinson, *op. cit.,* p. 247.

[20] Hazel W. Hertzberg, *Teaching Population Dynamics.* New York: Population Instructional Materials Project, Teachers Colloge, Columbia University, 1965.

[21] See Hertzberg, *op. cit.,* pp. 5–12.

[22] Roy Chung, *Space-Time Diffusion of the Transition Model: Twentieth Century Patterns.* Unpublished paper, presented at the annual meeting of the Population Association of America, New York City, April 30, 1966.

[23] See, for example: Helen McCracken Carpenter, ed., *Skills in Social Studies* (Washington, D. C.: National Council for the Social Studies, Twenty-Fourth Yearbook, 1953); William H. Hartley, ed., *Audio-Visual Materials and Methods in the Social Studies* (Washington, D. C.: National Council for the Social Studies, Eighteenth Yearbook, 1947); Preston E. James, *New Viewpoints in Geography* (Washington, D. C.: National Council for the Social Studies, Twenty-Ninth Yearbook, 1959); Zoe A. Thralls, *op. cit.*

[24] See especially "Visual Aids and Teaching Materials," starting on page 68 in the Annotated Bibliography.

[25] Detailed information on outline maps and raised relief maps is available from commercial map companies; see Annotated Bibliography.

[26] Stephen H. Spurr, *Photogrammetry and Photo Interpretation,* 2nd ed. New York: Ronald Press, 1960, pp. 13–15.

[27] *Ibid.,* pp. 111–113.

[28] For a sample, write to: Hubbard Scientific Company, Northbrook, Illinois, and to commercial map companies.

[29] For information concerning projection uses and operating methods and for addresses of projector suppliers, see James W. Brown, et al., *A. V. Instruction: Materials and Methods* (New York: McGraw-Hill, 1964).

[30] Two well-known producers of overhead projectional materials are the Technifax Corporation, Holyoke, Massachusetts, and 3M Minnesota Mining Company, Educational Services, St. Paul, Minnesota.

[31] Brown, *op. cit.,* p. 465.

[32] Allen K. Philbrick and Harold M. Mayer, "A Technique for Visual Examination of Association of Areal Patterns, *Journal of Geography,* 50: 367–373, December 1951.

[33] See Brown, *op. cit.,* Chapter 20, for a discussion of copying methods.

[34] For further information write: Eastman Kodak Co., Rochester, N. Y.